THE GREATEST GAME

The Ancyent & Healthfulle Exercyse of the Golff

THE GREATEST GAME

The Ancyent & Healthfulle Exercyse of the Golff

DODD & PURDIE

MacLean Dubois

This edition first published in Great Britain in 2010
by MacLean Dubois
Hillend House
Hillend
Edinburgh

Reprinted in 2010

ISBN 978-0-9514470-7-9

Text copyright © David Purdie, 2010

Illustrations copyright © Hugh Dodd, 2010

British Library Cataloguing-in-Publication Data

A catalogue record for this book is available on request
from the British Library

Design: Emma Quinn

Printed and bound in Malta by Gutenberg Press

CONTENTS

FOREWORD

There are many books on the subject of golf, but I suspect there have been none quite like this one. The game is governed by strict Rules and also by Laws inexplicable to science. Books, however, need no such regulation and it is refreshing to find the authors prepared to base historical statements on firm facts when available, and on equally firm powers of invention when not. They have attempted nothing less than to fill the many gaps in our knowledge of the game, and they have done so with scholarship, much humour and glorious illustration.

Playing golf can be a serious business, as I know, but the game has a healthy habit of standing back from time to time and taking a wry, sideways look at itself, at the incongruities of its institutions and the eccentricities of its devotees. This book does just that. No area of golf escapes the surgical probing of David Purdie's pen, or the equally deft touch of Hugh Dodd's paintbrush. The book takes us from the invention of the warning *Fore!*, apparently by the army of Imperial Rome, to the European Union's help with the banana slice, GPS-linked tagging of club members to combat slow play, and finally to the extraordinary assertion that Wm. Shakespeare Esq. was probably a strolling player in more senses than one...

But overall, what emerges is the authors' love of the game. It is a game which they both play and whose traditions we all cherish as the bedrock of one of the finest outdoor pursuits to have been conceived by the mind of Man; the indeed ancient & healthful exercise of the golf.

However, to describe it any further here would be, to misquote Mark Twain, a good read spoiled. Enjoy.

COLIN MONTGOMERIE

INTRODUCTION

The genesis of this book lies several years back in an original concept I had to depict and describe the 'types' and mannerisms of club golfers. Being of that noble (distinguished, venerable) breed myself, I knew there to be a wealth of idiosyncratic behaviour, ancient etiquette, eye-catching ties and apoplectic secretaries to draw on. Having recently completed a book on the racing world with the late, great, Jeffrey Bernard, the temptation to cast a lucid (watchful, sardonic) eye over my colleagues and competitors on the links was irresistible.

Hundreds of scraps of paper, sketches, drawings and pictures later, I had accumulated a sizeable portfolio on the subject, but as yet had no clear path to publication – words were not my forte and my pen kept drifting to my drawing board.

I have Jonathan Muirhead to thank for the happy coincidence that led me to the Great Trades Hall of Glasgow one late November evening to hear Professor David Purdie speak at the Incorporation of Skinners and Glovers. A brilliant speech exposing the vicissitudes of his early life on Prestwick's links and the vagaries of the game in general led me to suspect that his knowledge of the 'golfing man' was deep, and that he maintained a profound reverence for historical inaccuracy to boot. So, from after-dinner drinks to the links we continued...

Our conversation carried us across days and weeks, fairways, greens and 19th holes, as we explored our shared delight in all things golf; from the history of mashie-niblicks to ruminations on the 'Club Bore'. David's column on Major Warren-Dawlish for *Golf International* and my illustrations of modern day hackers merged perfectly, but by then Rembrandt had appeared on my board, and Shakespeare was just emerging...

Several lunches later we conceived of the idea to create a irreverent 'History of Golf' with a few modern archetypes thrown in for good measure. The fact that most of the known history of golf dates from the 1860's onwards did not deter us, and thus with impeccable research and application we have, I believe, arrived at a definitive version of events.

David's brilliant observations have brought the past to life, illuminating the murky depths of history and of members-only golf clubs. They have been a great joy and inspiration to work from and the pages have flown by, filled with his quick-fire humour and self-deprecating take on 'the greatest game' on earth. I can't think that the book would have evolved in any other way.

My apologies in advance if you should find a resemblance within these pages. True drawings can only come from nature – remind yourself that imitation is the finest form of flattery.

HUGH DODD

This book is dedicated
to all those who have ever
teed it up, anywhere.

A QUESTION OF DESIGN

The perennial debate on human origins divides humanity into two broad camps: the creationists and the evolutionaries or Darwinians. The former believe that, as described in Genesis, it was by divine command and in just six working days, that humanity emerged from the preceding Chaos. In contrast, the latter are convinced that if left alone for c. 13.5 billion years, the basic building block of the Universe, elemental hydrogen, will turn into people. This book will not take sides in the debate, but will advocate that if there is a Great Designer, then the design of *Homo sapiens* clearly has a specific purpose. Just what that purpose might be remains one of the most difficult and challenging questions for contemporary science.

Let us place ourselves in the position of intelligent aliens. Let us further suppose that after an almighty struggle, we have tractor-beamed this creature up to our cigar-shaped craft orbiting the Moon. We would ponder its extraordinary design and wonder what on earth was its purpose, on Earth? What was this creature *for*? Our Chief Observer's report might contain the following observations, ever mindful that form follows function.

 REPORT

The creature is topped, or rather headed, by a domed superstructure. This houses its central processing unit, and features no fewer than seven USB ports for data collection, one, for audio, on each side and five at the front for visual, nasal and oral inputs. It is thus absolutely focused on examining the terrain in front of it. Curiously, there is no rear-facing port, as if the creature were designed to be impervious to signals and cries from other creatures coming along behind.

The upper dome is supported by a column of thirty-three jointed vertebrae constituting a flexible trunk from which sprout a strong ribcage, a stout pelvis and four limbs with digital extremities. The ribcage protects such vital organs as the creature's pump or heart, and its bellows or lungs, while the pelvis shields its extraordinary reproductive apparatus. And thus, from a height of around one zaphod[1] the whole assemblage looks out upon the surface of its habitat. That very look, however, is the key to its purpose. For it is no ordinary gaze. It is the level, stereoscopic stare of the hunter.

---

1   Zaphod. The interstellar unit of measurement. *Circa* 6 feet. Believed to derive from Zaphod Beeblebrox, Galactic President. See; *The Hitchhiker's Guide to the Galaxy* (1979) by Douglas Adams. Also, the distance above which putt sinkings fall to < 30%.

REPORT

The creature's twin upper sockets deliver an asset required by all predators: the three-dimensional vision which supplies the distance and the angle of intercept to the target. Thus informed, it can now compute the best means of deploying its weaponry. Most interestingly, however, the creature has no *inbuilt* means of attack: it lacks horns, bears no fangs and sports no claws. It must, therefore, be in the missile business! But this simply begs the question. What is the projectile, how is it discharged – and at what?

To address these questions we must go, literally, back to the top. The domed skull is clearly a protective carrying-case for its necktop computer, or brain. This is essentially a workstation whose computational power allows the creature to process data from its *omni*-directional vision. This is provided by the universal joint linking spine with workstation. It provides full 180° lateral swivelling and full vertical nodding capability. However, there is one obvious disadvantage to such extreme head mobility. This is the difficulty which the creature must experience in trying to keep its dome and hence workstation *still*, during critical activities such as missile launches.

One of the creature's central functions now begins to emerge. It is clearly designed to observe and record the flight of objects launched by itself or others. Its necktop computer is powered to track a small flying object over considerable distances, even when it exhibits a wildly curving trajectory and comes to rest in deep vegetation. The workstation then instructs the creature to advance to the location, its bipedal striding gait permitting rapid progress across both rough and fair ways. It also permits walking backwards, a function which allows stereoscopic observation of whether creatures following behind are being held up.

Each upper limb articulates with the central trunk by a broad shouldered flange, manifestly to facilitate the carrying of either a collection of launch weapons or a container for such. However, it is the design of the extremity of the upper limb which is of surpassing interest. The key feature is that the shortest of the five digits is opposable. In other words it has a gripping function, an activity in which it may be joined by the other upper extremity for the purpose of swinging, brandishing or indeed throwing an implement or weapon.

We conclude that this creature was designed to stand holding a weapon and to swing it, utilising its flexible spine and shoulder as a pivot. Then, holding its domed computer-case rock steady, it uncoils to unleash a blow at a small but presumably aerodynamic object, whose flight its stereoscopic vision then tracks into the remote scenery. However, one great question remains. *Why?*

Back on Earth, we too are left with the central question of purpose behind the creation, or evolution, of our anatomical design. Here we must turn to anthropology and to the earliest specimens of primate hominids discovered along the eastern division of the Great Rift Valley system in Africa. The famous Laetoli footprints[2] discovered in Tanzania were made by an ancestor not dissimilar to ourselves, *Australopithecus afarensis*, and have been dated to c. 3.5 million years ago. A furrowed track paralleling the footprints was also present and had clearly been made by the dragging of an object carried by the larger of the two creatures in the group. This object was a club…

Research continues into our remotest forebears' lifestyle and activities. Of the latter, club wielding seems to have been one of the first to emerge in Africa, the continent in which *Homo sapiens* first appeared and from which we set out on our long journey. However, still unknown to us is the location of the grasslands where club swinging, object striking and related small missile launching first began. The hunt for it is known to science as the search for the Missing Links.

On the creationist side of the great debate, perhaps the answer to our functional design may lie in the earliest recorded poem on the subject, dating from the seventeenth century BC. It may reveal just what those flying objects were, whose trajectories we are clearly purposed to follow.

Discovered in Mesopotamia[3] and translated from the original Proto Indo-European by Prof. David Robertson of Edinburgh University, it reads:

> *In the Garden of Eden lay Adam*
> *Lasciviously gazing at Madam,*
> *And he cackled with mirth, 'cos in all of the Earth*
> *There were only two balls – and he had 'em!*

However, new insight on the actual goings-on in Eden came to light in, of all places, Ghent cathedral. Here in the shimmering glory that is the Van Eyck brothers' altarpiece, we see clearly that Eve is not holding an apple but a ball, and there is another out of sight in her left hand.[4] This discovery has, in turn, led to a critical re-examination of the poem by Dr Henry Rieckelman of Delaware State University, who has proposed an alternative translation of the celebrated verse, as follows:

> *In the Garden of Eden stood Adam*
> *Avariciously gazing at Madam;*
> *He'd his clubs – and a Game*
> *But one problem remained,*
> *There were only two balls – and **she** had 'em!*

---

2   Observed by the anthropologist Mary Leakey and colleagues in 1976 at Laetoli, Tanzania.

3   Lit. Between the Rivers. These are the Tigris and Euphrates in modern Iraq.

4   The Ghent Altarpiece. Dutch: *Het Lam Gods* or *The Lamb of God* is in St. Bavo Cathedral. Begun by Hubert, it was completed by his younger brother, Jan van Eyck, in 1432.

PAGANICA

s noted in the first chapter, the thunderous debate on the origins of Life on Earth divides humanity into two camps: the creators and the evolvers. Similarly, historians of golf divide into those who believe that it sprang fully formed from the links land of Scotland, and those who advocate its evolution from more primitive precursors. In his magisterial *Golf – Scotland's Game*, Dr. David Hamilton suggests that one of the game's antecedents was the Roman sport of *paganica*. This was a two thousand year old stick-and-ball affair in which wooden clubs were used to belt a leather ball stuffed with goose feathers. It was generally believed that *paganica* had originated in Rome itself, until the recent and sensational unearthing, in Pompeii, of an airtight sarcophagus. Inside was a skeleton clutching a papyrus containing a long-lost section of text from the *Histories* of the great Roman historian P. Cornelius Tacitus. And among them, *mirabile dictu*[1], was his account of the Imperial Roman Army's first attempt (the first of many) to subdue the Scots.

Forty years after the Roman invasion of Britannia (England) in AD 43 by the Emperor I Claudius, the Legions pushed on into Caledonia (Scotland) to straighten out the locals who had been refusing to be reasonable, i.e. submissive, and had been making offensive hand and lower body gestures at Roman outposts. In the summer of AD 83, the Roman general Julius Agricola swept up the eastern seaboard and brought the Caledonii, or Scots, and their Highland allies the Picti, or Picts, to battle at a place which Tacitus calls Mons Graupius. Scholars still dispute the location of this international strokeplay event, but the majority favour the Grampian mountain of Bennachie in Aberdeenshire. The Scots army was commanded by Calgacus – the word means 'swordsman' – who was the very first Scot to have a named identity. He was also the first chief of his race to persuade the shy and intensely artistic Picts to join a coalition against the march of imperial Rome.

The Picti – the Latin word means the painted ones – were experts in the arts of total-body painting and tattooing. They had also perfected, by means of hedgehog quills, the technique of body piercing. This was all very well, said Calgacus to the (literally) colourful Pictish King Brude, but how did they feel about *Roman* body piercing, and preferably with something more substantial, such as a spear? In the event, the Picts' military speciality turned out to be camouflage. Being essentially human artworks, their ability to paint themselves into the landscape and thus vanish proved to be a major reconnaissance asset. Indeed, so adept were the Picts at disguising themselves as trees, shrubs, granite boulders etc., that the appearance of any human-sized piece of vegetation such as a gorse bush or a large rock in the Roman army's path of advance would trigger a panicky volley of *pila*, or javelins, from the vanguard. Usually these missiles would simply bounce off the inanimate target, but every now and then it would be the target that bounced off, though not before delivering a shocking vignette of Roman sexual irregularities.

1 *Lat:* wonderful to relate.

Our knowledge of the Mons Graupius battle itself comes from the *Agricola*, a surviving monograph by Tacitus who also happened to be the son-in-law of the general. Before the battle, he describes how the Scots, lined up thirty thousand strong and painted head to toe with multicoloured woad, sang their tremendous battle hymn :

> Hello hello, how do youse do? We are the boys
> In red and blue and green and *look!* most every *hue,*
> And noo, we're gonnae *blooter* youse. Aye, *You!*

Calgacus then addressed the troops in what is the first recorded speech by any Scotsman; and it was a belter. After delivering a blistering critique of everything Roman from foreign policy to table manners he concluded, in Tacitus' Latin translation:

> *'Auferre, trucidare, rapere, falsis nominibus imperium atque,*
> *ubi solitudinem faciunt, pacem appellant'*
> ('They plunder, they slaughter and they steal, so they do, by the way.
> This they have the *nerve* to call Empire – *and,* where they've made
> a *total* shambles, they call it *Peace!* Aye, right.')

The battle began with a deluge of javelins, cabers and darts from the Scots, followed by a massed infantry charge straight at the legions. The assault was accompanied by the bellowing of carnyxes[2], the scream of bagpipes and the even louder screams of men in kilts charging without underwear across a field of waist-high thistles. Alas, it was to no avail. The veteran legionaries held the line, counterattacked, outflanked the Scots and, in an hour, it was all over. Ten thousand casualties lay on the field and a wounded Calgacus was a prisoner of Rome. Now, it is of great interest to read in the newly unearthed texts that, back in his camp, Agricola treated his noble captive with courtesy, giving him food and wine in the *praetorium*[3], and asking him for his *post-mortem* analysis of the battle.

Calgacus had no hesitation in laying the cause of defeat squarely at the door of *pagh'anicadh* – Latinised by Tacitus to *paganica* – which in the old Pictish language means 'golf'. The clash at Mons Graupius had itself clashed, apparently, with a major *paganica* tournament at St Andrews. The prizes, headed by an old mead jug, included a year's supply of woad and a sensational holy relic, a metatarsal bone from the left foot of St Andrew. These tremendous trophies had attracted a huge field which, to the fury of Calgacus, had denuded his army of many of its best strikers.

---

2   A fearsome bronze Celtic war trumpet, used between c. 300 BC and AD 200. It was held vertically, its mouth styled in the shape of a boar's head. Used to signal troops to charge, it was a serious wind instrument, i.e. guaranteed seriously to put the wind up the opposition.

3   *Lat:* The commanding officer's quarters.

St Andrew, incidentally, had been martyred some twenty years earlier in the reign of Nero at Patras in Greece, whence his bones had been secretly brought to the town of Muckross, Pictish for 'headland of swine'. The town promptly renamed itself St Andrews, later cunningly adding the strapline *Tigh na Pagh'anicadh* – the Home of Paganica. Calgacus told Agricola bitterly that he had attempted repeatedly to ban *paganica* – and also *naganica*, the legendary game of golf on horseback which gave rise to polo. This was in order to promote the traditional manly pursuits of Caledonia; catching the javelin, heading the shot and synchronised caber tossing.

With the campaigning season over, the Roman army went into its *hiberna* or winter quarters at Tibbermore near Perth. Calgacus, a scratch *paganicaster* himself, fashioned clubheads from beech and holly, shafts from ash or hazel and taught the Roman officers to play. Goose feathers for production of the original ball or 'feathery' were a problem until a Pict was caught disguised as a palisade post. Offered the choice of crucifixion or disguise as a mallard he opted for the latter, successfully luring geese to the nearby loch. Calgacus' club production, however, was not without subterfuge. Early one morning, the gate sentries discovered two of their number lying unconscious beside two broken drivers, but no Calgacus – or mallard.

With the coming of Spring, back to the Eternal City of Rome went Julius Agricola. With him went his staff, his clubs, balls and other trophies. He celebrated a Triumph and received a warm reception from the Emperor Domitian. And scarcely was his big day over when the Campus Martius (Field of Mars) by the Tiber came alive with the whack of Scots beech on Roman leather and with the first warning cries of *Foro!*[4] as misdirected featheries hurtled among citizens in the nearby Forum. And so, thanks again to Tacitus, the long-disputed origin of golf's classic warning cry is settled at last.

Meanwhile, back in Scotland the Roman army's Ninth Legion, the famous Legio IX *Hispana*, hunting for Calgacus, advanced into the Celtic twilight and, somewhere near Glasgow, vanished without trace from history. But that is another story...

HOME OF THE GAME

The Kingdom of Scotland emerged from the mists of pre-history in the mid-ninth century AD under King Kenneth MacAlpine. He united the warlike Scots, a Celtic race who had arrived three centuries earlier from Ireland, with the Picts, an artistic, sensitive and ancient people related to the Welsh. The ethnic melting pot continued to bubble and then boiled over with the arrival, on the eastern coasts of the British Isles, of an avalanche of Saxons and, most importantly, the Angles. The latter were a Germanic people from Angeln, now known as Schleswig-Holstein on the borders of Germany and Denmark. They were to give to their new home the name of *Angelonde*, later de-italicised and anglicised to England – the land of the Angles.

Now, as Euclid taught and any student of geometry knows, there are three different types of Angle. Consequently, these immigrants leapt ashore and fanned out in three geometrically opposed directions according to their Anglotype. The Acute Angles, a smart lot, remained on the rich farming land of East Anglia. In contrast, the Obtuse Angles, always reluctant to take advice, headed south to populate the London area where they are found to this day. Lastly, the Right Angles, as the name implies, cannily turned sharp right after landing and set off northwards in the general direction of Aberdeen. One of their Kings, Edwin, established a great hilltop fortress on the river Forth which he selfishly called Edwin's Burgh and which was to give its name to Scotland's capital city.

The ethnic cauldron of Scotland required only two further additions to make up the race which, fate had decreed, would produce the greatest field game conceived by Man. Now united, the Scots, Picts and the newly arrived Right Angles dealt quickly with the remaining pockets of Ancient Britons who were still moving arthritically about. They then found their path to the Hebrides and the Northern Isles of Orkney and Shetland blocked by the awesome military and naval power of the Vikings. After much ill-tempered shouting and several inconclusive battles, a *modus vivendi* was arrived at whereby the Vikings were allowed to keep the offshore Isles for four centuries. In return they grudgingly agreed to stop pillaging, raping and burning along the coasts of Scotland and promised to diversify into basket weaving, herring salting and voyaging elsewhere. This they did; to Iceland, Greenland and the Land Beyond, now identified as Massachusetts.

In Scotland, the newly united people thus combined the potent bloodlines of Ancient Briton, Anglo-Saxon, Celt, Pict and Viking. This gave the Scots their unique character mix of romantic idealism tempered with hard-headed money-making realism and an utter determination, later enshrined by the R&A in *Rule 13,* that the ball shall be played as it lies.

It also gave them a bloody-mindedness in argument and debate, brilliantly summed up in his book *Blandings Castle* by the great English golf writer P.G. Wodehouse, where it is drily observed: 'It is never difficult to distinguish between a Scotsman with a grievance – and a ray of sunshine.'

But the Scots had been given something else, something wonderful: the coastal linksland. A relic of the last Ice-age, the links was that strip of marginal land lying between the beaches and the arable fields, and good only for the grazing of sheep and rabbits and for the bleaching of cloth. With its short and hardy grasses, its fast-draining sandy subsoil and its picturesque dunes, the links was clearly designed for something else, for a purpose; but what? For centuries, strong hairy men sat on those dunes pondering the question. It is a credit to the Scots' native intelligence and lateral thinking that within a mere one thousand years they had figured out what that purpose was. It was – a game! However, first the southern neighbours had to be seen to, or rather seen off.

The Scots have a legend of the Missing Verses from the Book of Creation. It describes the archangel Gabriel gazing down in admiration on the newly-created Scotland. He wonders at the cloud-capped mountains, the fertile valleys, the salmon-filled rivers and those sixty billion barrels of oil thoughtfully slipped by a benign Providence under a North Sea bordered by glorious linksland. He asks: had The Almighty not been, well, laying it on a bit thick here?

'Not at all,' was the answer from On High. 'Just wait till you see the *neighbours* I'm giving them!'

The battle of Bannockburn on Midsummer's Day AD 1314 ended two decades of war with those neighbours and won the Scots their national independence. The wars had seen an alliance between Highlander and Lowlander and it was possibly from an amalgam of the old Highland game of *camanachd*, modified in the Lowlands by imported elements of the Dutch *kolf*, that the game we know as golf began to emerge. The Scots, at last, could lay down the war club and lift up the golf club. With the peace, came the Game.

The earliest golfing grounds – or greens as the courses were known – were located in or around the nation's capital, the prime of them being Leith Links, now a public park hard by the port of Edinburgh. However, scarcely had the game begun to take root in the sandy soil of the links when the warning beacons blazed again and the tocsin sounded the cry to arms – the Obtuse Angles were back! All over Scotland games had to be cancelled, golf club AGMs postponed, regional qualifying competitions abandoned. Back into lockers went putter and driver – and out again came broadsword and battleaxe. Up on the border at Chevy Chase the Earl of Douglas, commanding the army, said to his officers: 'I am told by our scouts that the English approach, thirty thousand strong. Gentlemen, we are but a small country. Where are we going to *bury* them?'

Meanwhile, back in Edinburgh, King James II was seriously worried about the national shortage of bowmen, an area in which the Angles were famously strong. He was less than amused to discover that his subjects were not using their free time as instructed, shooting at the butts and working on their archery. Instead, they were out on the links working on their controlled fades and greenside bunker recoveries. It was birdies and pars that were being shot. Feathery balls rather than feathered arrows were filling the air. That did it. A recently discovered early draft of the famous Act of the Scots Parliament of 1457 reads:

ACTE (Drafte)

*It is statutit and ordainit thatte ye Game of ye Golff – and of ye Futeballe – be utterlye cryed doun & not used, they being skaithfulle [1] to ye securitye of oure Realme... and thatte all men will practisse with speare & battleaxe, sworde & longbow – and **not** with dryver, irones or ye hatefulle lobbewedge. For ye shutyng of Englyshemen is mair necessitous by far than the shutying even of Eagyles...*

1 Harmfulle, perillous.

Permanent peace eventually came with the U.K. in the seventeenth century and the Home International matches now take place with just as much intensity, but rather less bloodshed, at such venues as Carnoustie and Birkdale, rather than at Bannockburn and Flodden. Some advocate dissolution of the Union. Most Scots, however, believe that it would be an act of criminal irresponsibility to deprive England of the steady stream of friendly co-operative shop stewards, articulate football managers, captains of industry, MPs (and PMs) which the canny northern Kingdom has propelled south over the centuries.

But canniness begins at home, as evidenced by an English visitor who entered the pro-shop of an Aberdeen club to find the pro answering a telephone call from a Member and saying wearily: 'I'm sorry Mr. McKenzie, but for the tenth time let me *assure* you that *no* peg tee of *that* description has been handed in *here*!'

The British Isles gave many sports to the world but among them were three great field games: England contributed cricket and football with its twin codes of soccer and rugby, while Scotland bestowed the golf. Each nation has nourished and enhanced the other and once united, the Jocks & the Angles of all three types were to achieve far more together than either could have achieved alone. But old attitudes die hard.

'My Scotland is indeed a land of noble and wild prospects.' James Boswell Esq. once observed to Dr Samuel Johnson, LLD, his friend and the subject of his great biography. 'Sir,' growled the sage of Lichfield, 'the noblest prospect that a Scotchman *ever* sees – is the high road that leads him into *England*!'

CHUI WAN

The Chinese game of *Chui Wan* (hit pellet – with stick) is without question a form of golf and appears on many images of the Imperial court during the Ming Dynasty (AD 1368 – 1644) An image of the Ming Emperor Xuanzong clearly illustrates that the game he is playing involves striking a stationary ball into a flagged hole and thus fulfills the central criteria for golf. The origins of *chui wan* remained a mystery to sinologists until recently, when the answer began to emerge from a most unexpected quarter. The flag shown in the Ming era images is strongly reminiscent of those used in fifteenth-century Scotland. Moreover, its triangular shape specifically locates it to the region of East Lothian where the game had begun a century before. But how could golf have made it from north-western Europe to China half a millennium ago? The problem seemed insoluble, until the recent discovery of the records of the remarkable fifteenth-century voyages of the great Chinese Admiral, Zheng He .

Born in 1371 in the Chinese province of Yunnan, Zheng became the trusted adviser to Emperor Zhu Di who, in 1402, had become the third of the Ming dynasty to occupy the imperial throne. Zheng He directed in person the Ming policy of using Chinese sea power as a means not only of defence but of exploration and territorial expansion. The huge junks of his imperial fleet had up to ten masts and were called treasure ships because of their immense value. Teak-decked and measuring up to 500 feet on the waterline, they had a beam of around 180 feet and a displacement of up to 3,600 tons. They contained waterproof bulkheads which could be flooded in heavy weather, providing additional ballast and hence stability – a feature later to be copied by European marine architects. There is evidence that some of Zheng's ships travelled westward beyond the Cape of Good Hope. In particular, the Venetian monk and cartographer Fra Mauro describes on his famous 1459 map, the penetration of 'A huge Junk from Asia' into the Atlantic Ocean in 1420.

Zheng He himself wrote of his travels on a tablet erected in Fujian in 1432 :

> *We have traversed more than 100,000 li*[1] *of immense*
> *water spaces and have beheld in the ocean huge waves*
> *like mountains rising in the sky. We have set eyes on*
> *barbarian regions far away hidden in a blue transparency*
> *of light vapours, traversing the waves as if we were*
> *treading a public thoroughfare*

The discovery and publication of the Chinese records of Zheng's voyages shed immediate light on a longstanding mystery of mediaeval times held in the General Register Office in Edinburgh. Scottish records of the period describe the sensational arrival off East Lothian of 'Ane great Shippe of Heathenes' who came ashore at Wester Dunes and tried to barter with the locals. The sudden appearance at this time of jade goods, ivory and artefacts of Ming provenance at Gullane and North Berwick gives credence to this. However the interview between the 'Captane of ye great Shippe' and the King's Sheriff of East Lothian, Sir Menzies Imlay, was difficult in the extreme.

The Sheriff, pointing to himself and using the Scots pronunciation of Menzies, said,

'I – am – Mingis.'

This produced looks of absolute incomprehension from the Chinese. The Sheriff tried again, this time shortening his name to the familiar 'Ming'[2].

'I – *Ming*!' he said. Immediate comprehension. Smiles all round. Zheng He beamed and bowed indicating that his entourage were also Ming. Pointing out to sea where the great Junk was anchored, he indicated that the *ship* was Ming. Visibly shaken by this, Imlay tried again;

'Me *Ming*. You…?'

'Aha!' said the Admiral, pointing to an banner depicting the Emperor. '*Me* no Ming – *he* Ming. Me *He*!'

Clearly this exchange was going nowhere fast, so Imlay showing the hospitality which continues to this day at Wester Dunes, invited his strange oriental guest to dine with him, while his men traded with the local townsfolk. The jade and other items which appear at this time were clearly bartered for local specialities among which would have been clubs, balls and the distinctive triangular flags of the links of East Lothian.

---

1   *Ca.* 30,000 miles.

2   Menzies is pronounced 'Mingis' in Scotland and may be shortened to Ming; e.g. Ming Campbell = The Rt. Hon. Sir Menzies Campbell QC, PC, aka Ming the Merciless, sometime leader of the Liberal Democrats in the House of Commons.

Having dined at Wester Dunes, the records state that Imlay invited Zheng He to partake of 'Ane Game of ye Gowffe upon ye Linkes'. Sadly, the result of the game is unrecorded. However, most intriguingly, the 10th hole of the great North Berwick links, the closest point to where Zheng He came ashore all those years ago, is to this day entitled 'Eastward Ho!' As the Chinese personal name He is actually pronounced in Mandarin as 'Ho' this fine hole serves as a living memento of that remarkable occasion.

Back in China the game was known as *chui wan* and developed along very different lines from that followed in its homeland. This was evident in the golf events staged at the 2008 Beijing Olympics at which the game was a 'Demonstration Event' prior to its attainment of full Olympic status in 2016 at Rio de Janeiro. In China, the golf events were watched, incredulously, by the R&A's official observer, Lord Fanshawe, at the new Jade Mandarin course at Jiangshan. Players were permitted to bring their own clubs but *not* their own balls. Identical balls were issued and these were of the new DL (Distance-Limited) variety which cannot hit beyond 275 yards. Players were also issued with identically sized Chinese caddies, each wearing what appeared to be a conical lampshade on his head. No verbal contact was permitted between player and caddy, all of whom were athletes capable of a sub-five minute mile, for reasons that will immediately become apparent.

The first event was the individual 36-hole Time Trial, won by the Australian Greg McDonald in a time of 1 hour 12 minutes 34.87 seconds. The fact that time counted, in addition to the score, was a completely new departure in golf. In the heats, Von Recklinghausen (Germany) displayed great athleticism in hitting powerful shots while actually running at full speed, but overran the 16th green and, unable to stop, sped on into the Bollinger Tent and failed to reappear. The final certainly provided great theatre as McDonald and Uzbekistan's Ugorokov raced down the 18th, played their approaches neck and neck, holed out and then sprinted the final 200 metres to the tape.

Even more dramatic was the next day's final of the Team Pursuit when the winners, Great Britain (Willis and Hathaway) starting at the 14th, succeeded in playing through no fewer than six other pairings between the Shotgun Start and the Hooter, one hour later. There was a disagreeable incident when Willis's drive felled Agostinio (Brazil) while overtaking his pairing on the 9th, mainly because shouts of *Fore!* had been banned by the Chinese due to the word's delicate gynaecological meaning in Mandarin.

The last Olympic competition in China was the synchronised golf. This was another new concept for competitors from the West, but proved to be one of remarkable aesthetic content and style. Teams of four players tee up and play, in perfect unison, a stroke with driver, then midiron and finally lobwedge, the balls being required to land within an area colour-coded like an archery target. Interestingly, players were not only to be identically dressed and coiffed but were also to make all shots while wearing the widest possible fixed smile. Points were awarded for technical merit and for artistic impression and there was a tariff, or scale of difficulty, based on distance and degree of bend.

Strokes ranged from the Straight Shot to the Fade, Pull, Draw and, remarkably, the Shank. Initial objections to the latter were rejected by the hosts who pointed out that *Shan-king* in Chinese means 'good shot'. The sight of the US and GB teams spending hours shanking away on the practice range while exhibiting fixed grins was simply remarkable, as was the effect on the Press Tent whose bar was unfortunately just to the right of the playing area. The Europeans scored well technically on the hook and especially the high-tariff *reverse* shank, but fell away badly on artistic impression compared to the oriental teams, whose matching hairstyles, makeup and dental work were simply streets ahead.

Handing over to the chairman of Royal St George's Golf Club in England, where the demonstration golf of the 30th Olympiad will be held in 2012, the hope was expressed that the final event, not included at Jiangshan, would be sandiron tossing, known in China as *Ping Fling*. However, as club throwing of any description tends to be rather frowned upon in England, the Sandwich sandwedge event may have to await more enlightened times.

However, the Chinese clearly have had the game for half a millennium or more. Where it came from had been anyone's guess – until publication of the voyages of Zheng He. Golf is now growing mightily in popularity in the Middle Kingdom[3] where its embodiment of the truly Confucian virtues of co-operation, justice and moderation are helping to bond the people of this ancient land to our ancient and indeed healthful game.

---

3 China is called *Zhōngguó* (Romanised to Jhongguo) in Mandarin Chinese. The term can be literally translated into English as the 'Middle Kingdom' or 'Central Kingdom' i.e. the nation at the centre of the world.

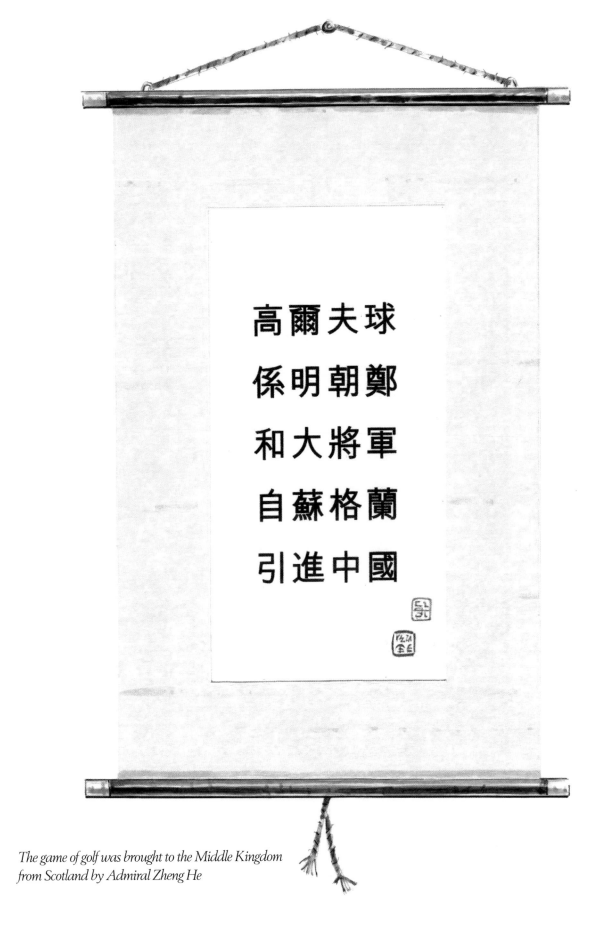

*The game of golf was brought to the Middle Kingdom
from Scotland by Admiral Zheng He*

MARY, QUEEN OF SCOTS (1542 – 1587) – GOLF FOR WOMEN!

Her Majesty Queen Marie Stuart, better known today as Mary Queen of Scots, has been generally regarded by historians as a tragic heroine and ultimately a victim of the ferocious religious and dynastic wars of the sixteenth century. It is only now, after scholarly examination of documents in the *Conciergerie* in Paris and in the Scottish Record Office in Edinburgh, that her true place as the Royal founder of women's golf has begun to be appreciated. We also have, at last, the answer to a centuries old golfing mystery. Why are ladies' tee boxes in Scotland universally coloured red?

The Queen's long and courageous campaign, first to establish the women's game in Scotland and then export it to England, was to lead to her exile and, in 1587, to her death warrant. This was signed by her cousin Elizabeth Tudor, better known as Good Queen Boss, the cricket enthusiast Queen Elizabeth I of England. Indeed, Mary's inability to keep her head down over the golf issue ultimately led to her inability to keep it on. The beheading of the 44-year-old Mary at Fotheringay Castle on the trumped up charge of plotting a *coup d'état* is now known to have been engineered by the *Mediaevael Crickette Cabale* (MCC) the governing body of English cricket, desperate to prevent the spread of golf south of the Border.

Born at Linlithgow in 1542, Mary was the grand-daughter of King James IV, a scratch golfer but high-handicap strategist. James felt that his marriage to Margaret Tudor, sister of the future Henry VIII of England, gave him the right to forcibly introduce golf south of the Border. This was a policy which had ended disastrously when he lost a major international strokeplay event – and his life – at Flodden in 1513. This defeat was a direct result of King James overturning an earlier ban on golf which had been seriously distracting the Scots from their archery – and from their traditional involvement in what may be politely described as the cross-border livestock transportation industry.

Mary had succeeded to the Scottish throne aged only six days, on the death of her father King James V. In 1548, now aged nearly six years, she was evacuated to France for safety from England's gigantic King Henry VIII who wanted her affianced to his son Prince Edward, junior President of the MCC. To draw attention to this proposal, an English army under the Earl of Hertford ravaged the Scottish Borders in what was known as the *Rough Wooing*, burning abbeys, pillaging golf clubs and enforcing cricket on a sullen and resentful population.

The French and the Scots artfully avoided a marriage with Edward by marrying Mary to the Dauphin[1] François. Meanwhile, in England, the accession of Elizabeth Tudor as Queen Elizabeth I meant that Mary, by virtue of her Tudor grandmother, was now next in line to the English throne. This title was indeed claimed for her by her father-in-law King Henry II of France whose death in 1559 brought the crown to François, who promptly died. Mary was now the widowed Queen of France – aged 18.

François had been a scratch handicap player of *jeu de mail* and had taught his sporty wife this cross-country stick-and-ball game which, along with *escargots bourguignonne* was a national obsession in France. Indeed he and Mary had sensationally won a playoff for the 1558 French *jeu de mail* mixed Open at Versailles. The French regarded this game as the direct ancestor of golf, rather to the irritation of their Scottish allies who dismissed *jeu de mail* as a type of hockey at best – and at worst little more than open-air billiards.

Mary returned to Scotland as Queen in 1561 and, for reasons still unclear, married her cousin Henry Stuart, Lord Darnley, a worthless rake and habitual shanker whose preferred venue for a mixed foursome was any bed except his own. The marriage did however produce an expert golfing prince who, much later as King James VI, was to unite the Crowns of Scotland and England, reducing his Royal numeral in the process to I and his handicap from X to V.

Relations between Mary and Darnley deteriorated sharply following the latter's shocking murder of David Rizzio, her Italian secretary and foursomes partner, and his flat refusal to propose Mary for Edinburgh's prestigious – and all male – *Burgess Golff Clubbe.* Shortly afterwards, Darnley was carousing in Kirk O' Field House while attempting a mercurial recovery from an attack of syphilis[2], when the house was blown to smithereens by a tremendous gunpowder explosion. The fact that Darnley's body was discovered outside the house, hands bound behind his back, led to his death being logged by the Edinburgh CSI team as *'suspicious'.* This view was reinforced when it was found that he had also managed to garrotte himself before, or after, tying himself up.

The Protestant reformation now being in full swing, Mary, a practising Roman Catholic, now ran into trouble with John Knox the most ferocious of the Calvinist reforming ministers and author of that famous polemic *'The first Blast of the Trumpet against the monstrous Regiment of Women.'* When Knox discovered that just four days after Darnley's death, Mary had been playing golf with the Earl of Bothwell on the links at Seton Sands just outside Edinburgh, his fury erupted[3]. It was widely rumoured that not only on the golf course was Mary being partnered by Bothwell, who was also suspected of placing the explosives – and the garrotte. In a two-hour sermon in St Giles Cathedral and in her presence, Mary was stigmatised as a daughter of Beelzebub, a scarlet woman of Babylon – and worse.

---

1 Fr. *Dauphin* – dolphin. The heir to the French throne was always a dolphin.

2 Mercury, or quicksilver, was an early treatment for syphilis. Hence the old planetary adage; *A night with Venus – and a lifetime with Mercury…*

3 Knox's fury often erupted. 'Child of the *Devil!*' he bellowed at his daughter as she came down late one morning for breakfast.
'Good morning, *Father*', the hussy replied.

'In God's name, Ma'am, is not he finyshed?' said the courtier Earl of Douglas, awakening from a sound sleep to find Knox thundering up to yet another climax.

'Verilie, my Lord, he is indeed *finyshed*,' said the witty Queen, 'but, alas, he cannot *stoppe...*'

Ignoring Knox and his ilk, Mary was regularly seen playing against lords, commons and foreign ambassadors either in a four-feathery, or a two-feathery foursome. Here she would be attended by her maids of honour the famous '*Four Maries*' of the folksong: Beaton, Seaton, Carmichael and Hamilton. These games took place on the ancient links of Bruntsfield, then outside Edinburgh, the beauty of the tall auburn-haired Queen and her maids ensuring huge galleries of appreciative spectators, held back by the pikes and halberds of the Bodyguard Royal.

The Golfing Ladies Union of Scotland traces its origins to this time and was granted a Charter by the Queen in 1567 to the utter fury of John Knox. His sermon '*The Second Blast of the Trumpet, this time against the monstrous Regiment's invasion of the Links*' was one of the provocations for the civil war which led to the final defeat of Mary's army at the battle of Langside and her subsequent flight into England and the tender mercies of Elizabeth.

The original male golfer has still not been identified. Whether it was a Caledonian chieftain on a Perthshire parkland or a shepherd on a Fife links, his name is lost to us. Not so for the ladies, since no woman before Mary Queen of Scots is known to have played the greatest game. Hence the founder of golf for the fair sex is a true Royal heroine whose name is not only known, but will live for as long as the game is played from Scotland's famous red ladies tee boxes. For these objects derive their colour from the tragic, ravishing and flame-haired Queen who took *Golf for Women!* from a mediaeval political crusade to the worldwide reality which it is today.

REMBRANDT, KOLF AND HOLLAND

Rembrandt, properly Rembrandt Harmenszoon van Rijn (1606 – 1669) was the pre-eminent painter and printmaker of the Golden Age of Dutch painting. Famous for his self-portraits and those of his contemporaries, he was also a master of biblical scenes but perhaps most importantly, he was a great golfing artist. There is but one picture in his entire *oeuvre* of a sportsman. This is *Die Kolver* (The Kolf Player) of 1654, now in the Boston Museum of Fine Arts, with its masterful use of chiaroscuro, that combination of light and darkness which is the hallmark of golf itself.

The player appears to be clad in plus-fours, waistcoat and a ten-gallon (45.5 litre) hat and to be carrying, rather than whacking, a huge kolfball. The player's klub is of a doubtful and possibly illegal design. Indeed it has the appearance more of a garden hoe or spade – a ditching rather than a pitching wedge and it would have been of keen interest to the R&A's splendidly named Balls & Implements Committee, had it been in existence. In the foreground can be seen another player who is either suffering from a seismic hangover or is clinically depressed. The identity of Rembrandt's *kolver* has never been known, but given that no artist painted more self-portraits than he, it is not unreasonable to assume that the player may be the great artist himself.

The year 1654 was a busy one for him. Around the time this etching was completed, his companion Hendrickje Stoffels gave birth to their daughter Cornelia and Rembrandt himself was in deep financial trouble possibly due to heavy losses at kolf which may, or may not, have arrived from Scotland centuries before. It certainly appears that over four hundred years ago Scots traders from Edinburgh were in Holland, flogging cleeks, mashies, niblicks, spoons, jiggers and other golfing impedimenta. Just after Rembrandt's *Die Kolver* appeared, the great Dutch poet Jan Six van Chandelier (1620 – 1695) was to reveal a fascinating Scots-Dutch connection in his poem *s'Amsterdammers Winter* published in 1657 in *Poesy*, his collected works. Here we find the Dutch kolf player wielding his *Schotse kliek,* that is, his Scottish cleek, which in the old Scots language was a long-range club equivalent to the modern 3 – 4 iron. So the Dutch were using Scots clubs half a millennium ago, which begs the question regarded with horror in the Netherlands – was the game actually a Scots import?

De kolver bindt zijn ijsspoor aan,	The Kolver binds his ice spurs on and
Of heeft iets strams om op te staan,	finds a rough place on which to stand,
Want 't gladde glas, is 't onbesneeuwd,	– for when slippery ice is free of snow
Met effe soolenlacht, en spreeuwt!	it laughs and scoffs at the smooth sole!
En naa het looten van paartij,	The sides being drawn, he stands secure
Schrapstaande slaat syn esp, met bly	and strikes forwards with his leaden ash,
Verswaart, of syne Schotse kliek,	or his Scottish cleek
Van palm, dry vingers breed, een dik	three fingers wide, one thick.

Another kolfer was Gerbrant Bredero, a much admired playwright of the Dutch Golden Age, who was also the *vaandrig* or standard bearer of the Amsterdam civic guard. In 1618 at the age of 33, Bredero died of pneumonia contracted from falling through the ice of a frozen canal, doubtless while playing *kolf*. For the Dutch certainly played a club and ball game both inland and on the ice-covered canals of the Netherlands during the Little Ice Age of the 1600s. The Dutch for a club is *kolf*, whose plural form, *kolven*, gave its name to the sport itself: *spel met kolven*, the game with clubs. The similarity between the *kolf* and the golf, like the propinquity of Scotland and Holland, is just too close to be accidental.

The game seems to have been popular with the artistic community. Reynier Vermeer, art-dealer father of the great painter Johannes Vermeer was hauled before the civic authorities in Delft to explain why a *kolf* match had ended in a brawl with knives drawn and casualties. Delft was also the scene of a tragedy for Rembrandt in the year of his *Die Kolver*. This was the death of his most gifted pupil Carel Fabritius, a casualty of the great Delft disaster of 1654. What happened apparently was that Cornelius Soetens, keeper of the city's gunpowder store, went down to inspect the forty tonnes of explosives in his charge, incautiously striking a match to light his pipe as he did so. The resulting gigantic blast was heard 150 kilometres away at Texel and did for poor Fabritius, many of his paintings, and indeed for most of Delft with its famous tiles, several of which were airmailed by the explosion as far as Cleethorpes in England.

However, the great central question remains: which way went the traffic? Did golf reach Holland from Scotland via our mediaeval traders, or did *kolf* disembark from Dutch merchant ships which habitually docked at Leith, which is the port of Edinburgh, with its Leith Links, thought to be the truly original golf course in Scotland. Thus we have Scottish golf clubs going to Holland and Dutch kolfballs being landed in Fife. We also have close affinity between both races in terms of language, with Old Scots and the Frisian tongue of western Holland being first cousins.

The key piece of evidence lies in the word itself. Dutch words entering English convert an initial 'k' to 'c'. Thus we have cruise from *kruisen*, cookie from *koekje*, coleslaw from *koolsla* and so on. Thus had our game arrived from the Netherlands it would have become *colf* rather than golf, which has had that initial 'g' from its first mention in the annals. Conversely, if an English word with an initial 'g' enters the Dutch language it tends to undergo a sound-shift whereby the 'g' is shifted to a 'k' since the Dutch have huge difficulties pronouncing the English hard 'g'. This is because they are programmed by their own splendidly complex guttural 'g' which sounds like a bronchitic sealion clearing its throat.

Hence the solution adopted by the highly practical Dutch was simply to replace the English initial 'g' with a 'k'. Thus *kolf* in Holland must originally have been golf, which places the game's origin securely in Scotland – for the moment. Whatever the truth, thanks to the great Rembrandt we can visualise a Dutch *kolfer* and his kaddy consulting the kard of the kourse and calculating the correct klub for the shot. There have, however, been occasions when Scotland and the Netherlands have traded shots of a more serious kind.

In Dundee, the fine parkland track of Camperdown Golf Club lies on the estate of Admiral Adam Duncan and is named after the Battle of Camperdown of October 1797. In this encounter Duncan's North Sea Squadron defeated a Dutch fleet which had been rented by France to escort the transports carrying a 50,000 strong French army on one of their regular attempts to invade the UK. Duncan, 6ft 5ins, and a keen golfer, captured the even larger Dutch Admiral J. W. de Winter (2.03 metres)[1] when the latter's flagship, the *Vrijheid* (74) struck her colours. He offered his sword to Duncan on the quarterdeck of his flagship HMS *Venerable* (also 74). Duncan, however, in true Scots golfing tradition and as if a game on the links was ending, told his opponent to keep his sword, doffed his hat and warmly shook his hand.

Having been brought ashore, conveyed to London and presented at court, de Winter was addressed by George III:

'Admiral, your fleet was found to be escorting a French army on its way to England. Now, we can quite understand the French, with whom we are at war, wishing to invade our realm, but we are not, to my knowledge, at war with Holland. Can you explain this seeming paradox?'

With a low bow, de Winter, commercially savvy like all his race, replied, 'We are *indeed* at peace with Great Britain, your Majesty, but business is *business*!'

History does not record if those two fine old seadogs ever played a round together in later years, but both were lucky to see the links again, given the bloodletting of the Camperdown battle when there were close to two thousand casualties.

'Indeed,' said de Winter later, 'it is a matter of marvel that two such gigantic objects as Admiral Duncan and myself should have escaped the carnage of that day.'

Peace reigns now across the waters of the North Sea and whether the game came from Holland to Scotland or *vice versa*, it remains a legacy to humanity from both nations, as does the genius of Rembrandt in his depictions of himself, his country and his compatriots – with their great *spel met kolven* – the game with the clubs.

---

1   6ft. 8ins.

Mr. WILLIAM
SHAKESPEARES

COMEDIES,
HISTORIES & GOLFEING,
TRAGEDIES.

Publifhed according to the True Originall Copies.

Martin Droeshout sculpsit London.

LONDON

Printed by Ifaac Iaggard, and Ed. Blount. 1623.

To his moft gracious Majefty, King James, patron of the Gentleman golfers of Black Heathe, this volume is dedicated by his Majefty's loyal fervant, Will Sheakfpeare.

WILLIAM SHAKESPEARE
A STROLLING PLAYER...

We know so little about the private and sporting life of the Bard of Avon, that it is from the texts of his thirty seven plays and 154 sonnets that we source much of our information on his personal pursuits and opinions. There has been great speculation and much wild conjecturing on the subject of Shakespeare's extra-theatrical activities. When resting between performances he has been accused of complicity in everything from mediaeval football to real tennis and bear-baiting, usually on the flimsiest evidence. However, the advent of computerised concordances together with careful textual analyses of the *First Folio* edition of the plays of 1623, point to the inescapable conclusion that the man was a golfer. This is perhaps not too surprising since he was right there, at the Globe Theatre at Southwark, when a great show opened in London. This was the all-new Stuart Dynasty no less, starring James Stuart with Anne of Denmark as his leading lady. It came with a cast of scores of Scots, and with them came a new game.

In March 1603, when Shakespeare was 39, a very dusty Sir Robert Carey had arrived in Edinburgh non-stop from London on an exhausted and furious horse. He marched into the Palace of Holyroodhouse demanding an audience with the monarch and was promptly thrown out again by the seneschals with a growled, 'Ye Kyng is atte ye Golff'. Directed to the links of Musselburgh, he eventually found King James VI in deep rough to the right of the 5th fairway. Falling to his knees, Carey broke the news that Good Queen Bess was no more, that James had shot up from VI to I on the new UK leaderboard and would soon be exchanging the hickory shafted mashie in his hand for a rather larger sceptre.

Thus the demise of the Tudor regime heralded the advent not only of the Stuarts but also of golf in England. Down to London with their new, improved sovereign went a vast crowd of Scotsmen on the make, among them William Mayne, 'Hys Majestie's clubbe & balle maker' and before long golf on the Black Heath, close to the royal residence of Eltham Palace, was a regular pastime of the court. Indeed the Royal Blackheath Golf Club dates its foundation to this era, and celebrated the quatercentenary of the Blackheath *Goffer* in 2008.

Over at Southwark, the Globe Theatre's actors and their master dramatist, finding themselves now under royal patronage, smartly changed their name from the Lord Chamberlain's Men to the King's Men. One of the first plays of the new era was *Macbeth* in which Will himself astutely took the role of Banquo, a canny move since King James firmly believed the royal Stuarts to be descended from Macbeth's friend and victim. In a famous scene in Act IV, Shakespeare has the witches, those 'foul and midnight hags' show Macbeth a procession of future kings. The eighth of these is James himself who appears holding a triple sceptre representing the new, expanded U.K., and carrying 'balls'. We are not told explicitly that these were golf balls, but this is most likely, given that golf was the King's outdoor ball game and the hags were operating their cauldron on what is now the 14th fairway of Brora Golf Club. It is likely that Shakespeare would have gone up to Scotland while researching *Macbeth*, where he would have played on the great links at Dornoch and Cruden Bay. Certainly golfing images abound in his plays and sonnets. In *Titus Andronicus* we hear Quintus lamenting the rudimentary greenkeeping on early seventeenth century courses. He arrives on a tee and grimly surveys what lies ahead:

What subtle hole is this, cover'd with rude-growing briers,
Upon whose leaves are drops of new-shed blood
A very fatal place it seems to me.

In *All's Well That Ends Well*, Bertram's friend Parolles gives vent to the eternal complaint of links players as the ball lands on the fairway, but kicks hard sideways into the rough; *'Why, these balls bound, 'tis hard.'* It is indeed.

Henry V, heading for France again and yet another strokeplay encounter with the Dauphin, displays the positive approach needed in international matches and known as 'attitoode' by our American cousins:

We, in France, by God's grace
Shall strike his father's crown into the Hazard... but whether this is a water hazard or just the royal bunker is left unsaid.

In the poem 'A Lover's Complaint' we hear the classic story of players about to drive who are distracted or 'diverted' as Shakespeare calls it, with the usual result that their drives skitter along the ground. It was never better put than this:

As they did Battery to the spheres intend;
Sometime diverted – their poor balls are tied
To the orbed earth.

How regrettable that our modern English has moved on from this glorious language to the arid techno-speak of the present day. The caddy, asked by the player where on earth his drive has gone, will no longer say, 'Sir, it rose not, neither did it fly, but briefly scuttled as it hugged the jealous ground. A poor ball, Sir. Yonder it lies – tied to the orbed earth...'

As he was an aesthete, we should not be surprised to find that Shakespeare was a critical judge not only of quality of play but also of swing action. In *Troilus and Cressida* we encounter the warrior Ajax, son of Telamon and second only to Achilles in the Greek pantheon of heroes. Interestingly, he is being praised by Odysseus for his *'Great swing, and rudeness of his poise...'*

It is truly fascinating to hear that Ajax had a great swing, however rude (i.e. crude) his poise at address. There is absolutely nothing in the text of the *Iliad*, Homer's account of the Trojan War, to suggest that those great swingers Ajax, Achilles, Hector or indeed anyone on either side, played golf in the intervals between the slaughter. Further research is clearly required here.

Similarly, in *Antony and Cleopatra* it is astonishing to hear Lepidus saying to Octavius Caesar: *'Let all the number of the stars give light to thy fairway...'* The fact that young Octavian, great-nephew of Julius Caesar and the future Emperor Augustus, needed starlight to go about his business on the fairway illustrates the tremendous energy of the man. He governed the great Empire by day, and he smacked it round at night.

Golf clubs, using their original names, feature strongly in the Works. *'Your belly is all putter'*, says Sir Hugh Evans to Falstaff in Act V of *The Merry Wives of Windsor*, thus proving that there is nothing new in the controversial extended putter.

The famous old fairway club, now simply the 3-wood but known for centuries in Scotland as the Long Spoon, turns up in Act II of *The Tempest*. *'I have no long spoon!'* laments Stephano, clearly caught out with 220 yards to go to the green and the Rescue Club four centuries in the future.

But we finish where we began, with the Scottish play. Macbeth, the eponymous monarch is clearly a poor player. At the end, dormy 6-down to Malcolm and Macduff, he sadly mutters to his attendant words which are echoed on 18th greens to this very day. Slowly, resignedly, putting the putter back in the bag for the last time after a series of disasters, Shakespeare has him intone words which he himself might have cried to the heavens after one last missed 3-footer on the 18th at Blackheath:

'Out, out, brief candle! Life's but a walking shadow, a poor player who struts his hours upon the stage – and then is heard no more...'

Exit (pursued by caddy for payment).

LEITH LINKS & *The Rules*

Bordering the great port of Edinburgh at Leith is the fine public park known to this day as Leith Links. This is holy ground for golfers, as many historians believe that it may well be the oldest golfing ground, or 'green' to use the old Scots term for it, which can be identified. It is not the oldest currently working golf course, however, that honour lying with Musselburgh Old, a few miles down the coast. The links was once the golfing playground of King Charles I, and it was while actually playing here in 1641 that the monarch received news of yet another Irish rebellion. Here also the first international foursome took place when James, Duke of York and brother of the king, was partnered by John Patersone, one of Edinburgh's best players, and took the money off two visiting English aristocrats.

Leith Links is still a place of recreation for citizens with its football, rugby and cricket pitches, public footpaths and allotments. Golf is still played occasionally, when the original five holes are recreated and played over, using hickory clubs and oldish balls, by the splendid Leith Rules Golf Society. Their very name reflects the fact that the Links was the scene of one of the most momentous events in the history of the game.

Here on Leith Links the Rules of Golf, described initially as *Articles & Laws,* were first codified in the year 1744 and, most importantly, written down. Obviously there must have been informal regulations to control matches prior to this and to settle disputes and duels, but it had clearly become necessary to arrive at a unified set of rules before there were any more deaths.

The body responsible for golf's initial legislation were *The Gentlemen Golfers* who, in 1744, were presented by the Town Council of Edinburgh with a silver club to be played for annually in a competition. As this would be open to non-members, written rules would be required. The winner of the competition would become Captain of the Gentlemen Golfers for the following year and would affix a silver ball bearing his name to the silver club. The first to do so was John Rattray, surgeon, who also signed his name to the first set of the Rules. The Town Council's prize is strongly reminiscent of the Silver Arrow presented as a competition prize in 1709 to the Royal Company of Archers, the Monarch's bodyguard in Scotland. Golfers were also required by the Council to wear a red jacket to identify themselves and thus warn non-golfing citizens to take cover, much as a mandatory red flag would later be waved ahead of advancing horseless carriages – and Marxists.

At the time in question Leith was not, as now, joined to the city of Edinburgh. It was a wealthy and independent town, the home of prosperous merchants and professional men servicing Scotland's trade with continental Europe. Golf was then a winter game played by the middle and upper classes and royalty who could afford the equipment and the expensive feathery balls.

In that era, the aristocracy and gentry would spend the Spring and Summer on their country estates until the harvest was in, coming to the capital for the winter social season. There was also a greenkeeping reason. Before the advent of mowing equipment the grass on the 'greens' was just too long for practical play and the golfing season would extend, effectively, for the six months from October to March. The writer Tobias Smollett described in one of his novels the scene on Leith Links where, armed with horn-tipped 'bats' and balls of leather stuffed with feathers, the players would 'strike with such force & dexterity that the ball will fly to an incredible distance.'[1]

The Gentlemen Golfers were later to migrate from their home on Leith Links, first to Musselburgh in 1836 and, over fifty years later, to their magnificent links of Muirfield in East Lothian. Entitled since 1800 The Honourable Company of Edinburgh Golfers, they preside over one of the finest championship courses on earth – and indubitably over the best lunch in golf.

Articles & Laws in Playing at Golf   *7th March 1744*

1. You must Tee your Ball within a Club's length of the Hole.

2. Your Tee must be upon the Ground.

3. You are not to change the Ball which you Strike off the Tee.

4. You are not to remove, Stones, Bones or any Break Club, for the sake of playing your Ball, Except upon the fair Green & that only within a Club's length of your Ball.

5. If your Ball comes among Watter or any wattery filth, you are at liberty to take out your Ball & bringing it behind the hazard &Teeing it, you may play it with any Club & allow your Adversary a Stroke for so getting out your Ball.

6. If your Balls be found any where touching one another, You are to lift the first Ball, till you play the last.

7. At Holling, you are to play your Ball honestly for the Hole, and, not to play upon your Adversary's Ball not lying in your way to the Hole.

8. If you should lose your Ball, by it's being taken up, or any other way, you are to go back to the Spot where you struck last, & drop another Ball, And allow your adversary a Stroke for the misfortune.

9. No man at Holling his Ball, is to be allowed, to mark his way to the Hole with his Club, or anything else.

10. If a Ball be stopp'd by any person, Horse, Dog, or any thing else, The Ball so stop'd must be play'd, where it lyes.

11. If you draw your Club in order to Strike & proceed so far in the Stroke as to be bringing down your Club; If then, your Club shall, break, in any way, it is to be Accounted a Stroke.

12. He, whose Ball lyes farthest from the Hole is obliged to play first.

13. Neither Trench, Ditch or Dyke, made for the Preservation of the Links, nor the Scholar's Holes or the Soldier's Lines, shall be accounted a Hazard; But the Ball is to be taken out / Teed / & play'd with any Iron Club.

John Rattray, Capt

---

1   T. Smollett, *The Expedition of Humphrey Clinker*, 1771.

The Rules, which are now administered by the R&A and the USGA, have obviously undergone much expansion, complication and revision over the intervening centuries. However, it can be clearly seen that the central tenets of the game were in place from the very beginning: if your club shatters on the downswing – tough; whacking your opponent's ball with your own is not on; neither is slipping a new feathery down the trouser leg; watter (sic) and especially *wattery* filth are to be avoided, while military encampments, despite the presence of high-explosives, are apparently non-hazardous.

Perhaps the most interesting of the original Rules is No. 2, enacting that your tee *must be on the ground*. This may sound odd to modern ears until it is realised that this is a prohibition of the former practice of teeing it up on such useful structures as an upturned ale tankard, an egg-cup, or the head of your recumbent caddy.

However, perhaps the two most iconic legal features of the game had their first formal presentation at Leith Links all those years ago: the ball farthest from the hole shall be played first – and that ball, together with every other ball on every golf course in the Universe shall be played *as it lies*.

The first winner of the silver club competition was Dr. John Rattray, an Edinburgh surgeon of renown who, less than a year later, was to join the 1745 Jacobite rising led by the young pretender, Prince Charles Edward Stuart. Rattray was captured after Culloden and sentenced to hang for treason, only to be sprung from durance vile by his loyalist friend Lord Duncan Forbes. The latter was President of the Court of Session, Scotland's supreme court and a fellow member of the Gentlemen Golfers.

Thus did the great park of Leith take its place as the primal known site of the greatest game. And should you meet with those who have played the famous five holes with the Leith Rules Golfing Society, stand back in awe and, with apologies to Samuel Taylor Coleridge:

> *Weave a circle round them thrice*
> *And in rapture bow your head,*
> *For in Elysium they've fed*
> *And walked the turf of Paradise.*

GOLF: THE BALLOON GOES UP

Ballooning and golf have had an interesting relationship beginning even before the game itself began to balloon in the late nineteenth century. It began with the Montgolfier brothers, Joseph-Michel (1740 – 1810) and Jacques-Étienne (1745 – 1799) who came from the Ardèche in France and were the inventors of the hot-air balloon, or *globe aérostatique*. As the name suggests, the ancient family estate of Montgolfier (lit. the hill with the golfcourse) may have been the original home of golf in France.

During the Napoleonic unpleasantness, the French were keen to capture the strategic British fortress of Gibraltar which was proving impregnable to land and sea assaults. Reasoning that the only way in would be by air, the Montgolfiers designed and built a prototype troop-carrying balloon, the *Aerostat Réveillon* which was first flown with living creatures aboard in 1783. Interestingly, the test pilot was a sheep called *Montauciel*, or climb-to-the-sky, accompanied by a duck and a hugely symbolic cock, the last being the national symbol of France. The absence of a human pilot was due to an initial lack of interest among the French, most of whom regarded the ideas of *les frères Montgolfier* as so much hot air. However, later that year a successful first manned ascent took place from the Bois de Boulogne, in the presence of Louis XVI. The king had initially wanted the balloon crewed by two condemned criminals, who took one look at the balloon and its flight-plan and fell to their knees begging for the guillotine.

Meanwhile, up north in the home of golf, something was stirring on, or rather off, the ground. William Tytler, golfer, eccentric editor of the *Encyclopaedia Britannica* and friend of the poet Burns, had read about the Montgolfiers' experiments. In 1784 he tried it himself with 'The Grand Edinburgh Fire Balloon' whose brisk ascent, immediate descent and tremendous crash constituted the first aerial flight in the UK. His exploits, were however, eclipsed by the arrival in the city of a man who was to become one of the greatest names in ballooning, Signor Vincente Lunardi. In October 1785 a large and excited crowd filled the grounds of George Heriot's School in Edinburgh to see Lunardi's hydrogen-filled balloon take off and be propelled away towards Fife by the south-westerly wind.

The scene now shifts to the then newly formed (1784) Crail Golf Club. Seventh oldest in the world, the club is located on Balcomie Links in Fife and is north-east of Edinburgh. The members knew this. What they did not know was that aerial transportation was possible, let alone that it had arrived and was heading their way. Play was also under way in the club's October Monthly Medal competition when a small round object, initially the size of a gnat, was spotted approaching from the south-west. To the golfers' amazement and growing alarm, it grew rapidly to the size of a gigantic bumblebee as it silently bore down upon them.

Scattering into deep rough, bunkers, and in several cases over a cliff onto the beach, the members fell to their knees praying for forgiveness of past sins on and off the course. The supplications rose to a crescendo when, as the object passed low overhead, they spotted a figure, reasonably assumed to be the Archangel Gabriel, leaning over the side of the basket and addressing them urgently through a megaphone.

'Where art thou, good people?' Lunardi, now hopelessly lost, shouted down to a fourball kneeling abjectly on a fairway.

'We are on the 9th, Blessed One,' yelled back the bravest of the four, thereby only adding to the confusion overhead.

'But what lieth ahead?' came the cry from above.

'If *thou* knowest not, what hope have we?' was the despairing response from below as the balloon, now losing altitude fast, disappeared in the general direction of St Andrews, some ten miles distant.

Over two centuries later in 2002, a hot-air balloon unexpectedly hit the golfing headlines again, when something unexpectedly hit a balloon. This occurred in England at Royal St Luke's Golf Club in Suffolk venue of one of the RFQ (Regional Final Qualifying) events for that year's Open Championship at Muirfield. One week after the RFQ, the club's secretary, Maj. R.J.M. Warren-Dawlish MC, received the following letter from Lord Fanshawe, then President of the R&A.

Royal & Ancient Clubhouse
St. Andrew's
Fife, Scotland
KA3 4RY

My Dear Warren-Dawlish;

Thank you so much, old boy, for delivering such a jolly good RFQ at St Luke's – and pray convey to your staff our warm appreciation for all the hard work. However, there's a small fly in the ointment. We, as the Tournament organisers, have been served with a writ for damages by lawyers representing a Mr Sean Graham of the Suffolk Hot-Air Ballooning Club. It seems that, due to an unexpected shift of wind direction, Mr Graham's balloon, shaped apparently like a giant condiment bottle and emblazoned 'Ramage's Brown Sauces' drifted low across the course just as play began. While Mr Graham was attempting to regain altitude by jettisoning ballast, he alleges that he became aware of a running figure below who repeatedly shouted and gesticulated up at him. This figure was tall and burly, wore a Panama hat and plus fours, and was carrying what Mr Graham initially believed to be a shooting stick.

The figure, still running and looking up, then fell head over heels through a gorse bush and into a bunker. Thereupon, alleges Mr Graham, there was a loud bang from below and his basket, balloon and bottom were peppered with buckshot.

He has submitted several colour, close-up photographs of his backside taken later at the A&E Dept. of Suffolk Infirmary which seem, prima facie, to confirm this. Apparently the now punctured balloon leaked so much gas that its equally punctured pilot had to make an emergency descent into Waveney Marsh, where a hard landing did nothing for his posterior injuries.

We understand that repairs to the balloon (and to Mr Graham) will be expensive and that we are to be the subject of proceedings under, of all things, the wartime Anti-Aircraft Artillery (Emergency Regulations) Act of 1940. This would be the first such action in peacetime and, as you'll appreciate, is highly embarrassing to the R&A.

I therefore asked one of our Members, Air Marshal Sir Digby Gardiner, how we should respond. His opinion is that a hot-air balloon, even if it looks like a sauce bottle, a sparkplug or even a giant diaper or nappy, actually is an Aircraft under the terms of the Act – and it is illegal to open fire on it, unless it has clearly shown 'hostile intent'.

We are thus in the difficult position of either paying compensation quietly to Mr. Graham, or going to Court to show that we believed ourselves to be under attack by a flying sauce bottle. The press will have a field day.

Finally, since the description of the anti-aircraft shotgunner bears a remarkable similarity to yourself, perhaps you might favour us with your version of events?

Yours ever,
Fanshawe

ROYAL ST LUKE'S GOLF CLUB (EST.1603)
From: *The Secretary*

Royal St Luke's Clubhouse
Carrington Magna, Suffolk
SU3 1GC

My Dear Fanny,

What happened was this. I had been out on the course early with Williams, looking for duck with a pair of 12-bores, when I saw the most extraordinary thing I've ever seen on a golf course. Over the hill to the landward side of the 14th rose a bloody great sauce bottle. Williams saw it first and was swearing never to touch drink again when I told him to shut up, because I could now see it too. Suddenly, out of a basket hanging below the bottle there came whistling down a stream of bags of wet sand. I suppose in retrospect it was the balloonist chap tipping out the ballast, but in these circumstances one's military training takes over. I shouted, 'Take *cover*!' and released the safety catch on the shotgun.

We were clearly under attack.

You can imagine the effect of 50 pound weights being dropped from over 100 feet. The first one burst among the greenkeepers on the 12th green, the second went clean through the roof of a (Ladies) Portaloo and the next landed right in front of J.C. Masterman of Sunningdale who was in the act of playing a shot. His ball went straight into the sandbag, followed by his 5-iron which broke and Masterman is now in dispute with the R&A Rules Committee as to whether a wet sand bomb is, or is not, an Outside Agency. That aside, I kept pace with the thing which was now down to about 50 feet, shouting up at the chap to clear off. In response there was a deafening roar as he fired up some enormous Primus stove-like flamethrower thing in the basket. At this point I fell over backwards into a bunker and the shotgun went off, just missing Williams but sending a double blast of shot up into balloon and basket.

He may sue us if he wishes but I will argue that the thing was clearly displaying hostile intent and I can tell you right now that we will be countersuing Ramage's Sauces for repairs to our bombed Portaloo. Incidentally, Jack Masterman's a barrister and may well be the very man to act for us. So, see you in court – and at Muirfield.

Yours ever,
RJM Warren-Dawlish, Secretary

GOLF GOES WEST:
THE AMERICAS

Just as in Europe, golf may have been preceded by *kolf* in the Americas, the game of the Scots following that of the Dutch into the New World. The first reference to the game comes from Fort Oranje (Fort Orange) Holland's first permanent colony in New Netherland. Named after the Dutch royal house of Orange-Nassau, it was located on the Hudson river on the site of the present day city of Albany, NY.

Kolf was causing trouble, again. In December 1659, the magistrates of Fort Orange had issued the following stern interdict:

Having heard divers complaints from the Burghers of this place against the practice of playing kolf along the streets, which causes great damage to the windows of the houses, and also exposes people to the dangers of being injured... their Honours, wishing to prevent the same, hereby forbid all persons to play kolf in the streets, under the penalty of forfeiture of 25 Florins for each person who shall be found doing so.

This was apparently the 'short game' played with such gusto and attended by fights, structural damage and general civic disorder in Holland. It was not the 'long game' of the Scots, the true ancestor of the modern game. Clearly *kolf* had been there from the start at Fort Orange, founded in 1624, but after thirty-five years of it, the *burgemeester* and his *magistraaten* had clearly had enough.

It was to be over a century later that golf appeared in the same area. In April 1779, with the United States now in being, an issue of *The Royal Gazette* in New York City carried an advertisement for 'Play-clubs¹ and featheries from Scotland'. Nevertheless it was to be a further century before the USA heard the first sound of *'Fore!'* coming from a certain cow pasture at Yonkers, NY and heralding the arrival of the Apple Tree gang and their St Andrews Golf Club. From that cow pasture was to spring the most powerful force in the golfing world. However, it had all begun far to the southward, in the Carolinas.

We do not know with certainty when or where the first Scottish play-club swept down from an American sky to send the first Scottish feathery ball on its way across a South Carolina links. Neither do we know who held that club or where he came from, but we can make an educated guess.

During the eighteenth century thousands of Scots packed up and headed westward to a hopefully better life in the Americas. The main destinations for the emigrants were the St Lawrence river as the gateway to Canada and the southern colonies of Georgia and the Carolinas in what was then British North America. With them into the holds of the terrible emigrant ships went their wives, children, ministers, swords, guns, attitudes and their love of a certain ancient game.

---

1   Drivers.

One of the principal arrival ports for the Scots was Charleston, South Carolina, and it was thither in 1743 that the sailing ship *Magdalena,* Capt. William Carse commanding, set sail from Leith, then as now the port of Edinburgh. Her berth would have been less than a mile from Leith Links, the true home of golf and where, just one year after she left for the New World, the first codified set of the Rules of Golf would be published. The *Magdalena* arrived in Charleston in August 1743 where shortly thereafter the mercantile firm of Stead & Evance were advertising in the *South-Carolina Gazette* the sale of merchandise from Scotland.[3] These may have been part of a shipment ordered by David Deas, a Scottish emigrant and successful merchant who was also a Provincial Grand Master of the Masonic Order. There is also evidence from later ships' manifests of consignments of golf equipment going to the more northerly colonies of Virginia in the 1750s and to Maryland a decade later.[4]

These Scots emigrants were to contribute mightily to the commercial and political life of the thirteen colonies and to the Revolution when it began in 1774. For example, Alexander Purdie migrated in the 1760s from Edinburgh to Williamsburg, Va., where he edited the *Virginia Gazette.* A committed revolutionary, Purdie's inflammatory organ published in 1773 a fiery essay by Sam Adams who had just led the Boston Tea Party. In this piece, Adams raised the great revolutionary cry of 'No taxation without representation!' and called for a Continental Congress of all thirteen colonies to discuss their grievances against the King. Adams and his firebrand friends knew that there would be no revolution without the Virginians whose colony was then the most populous and most economically developed. Thus, had it not been for Alex. Purdie's powerful sounding of the tocsin of revolt to engage the Virginians for the cause, there might have been no Congress, no Declaration of Independence and the author's family therefore must, with humble pride, assume responsibility for the United States.

However, to return to the good ship *Magdalena* and her cargo of salt, sailcloth and golf. Her manifest declares that she embarked '8 doz. clubs & three gross balls'. For the unwary, the latter does not refer to three overlarge balls, but to no fewer than three dozen dozen i.e. 432 featheries which accompanied the 96 clubs. This would have been sufficient to equip a dozen competent golfers for a decade, or a score of hackers for a fortnight.

Golf was played on Harleston's Green, then on the outskirts of Charleston but which is now in the heart of the city near the campus of the present College of Charleston. By the 1780s the members, mostly merchants, of the South Carolina Golf Club[5] would convene at John Williams' 'Carolina Coffee House' at two of the clock precisely. There they would dine and then proceed to the Green for the games of their Spring and Autumn meetings, the game as in Scotland being periodical to accommodate the growing season and the harvest. This famous city thus has the honour of hosting the first golfing society in the Americas, 130 years before the establishment of the first golf club on the continent whose records would survive.

---

3   Dr Nicholas Butler, Manager, the Charleston Archive, personal communication.
4   See *Golf* by David Stirk. Phaidon Press Ltd., London, 1987, pp 73 – 6.
5   See; C. Price and G.C.Rogers. *The Carolina Low Country; Birthplace of American Golf* (Charleston, 1980).

That club was Royal Montreal Golf Club, founded in 1873 in a dockside office by a group of eight Scots-Canadian gentlemen. Their leader, and the club's first Captain, was 52 year-old Alexander Dennistoun, originally from Dumbarton on the River Clyde, who had arrived in Quebec some ten years earlier. He was also their first President and lived to see the granting of the royal accolade by Queen Victoria. The members, following the tradition of the golfing pioneers back home, wore red jackets on the course which was originally just nine holes on Fletcher's Field, then on the outskirts of Montreal. Located now at Ile Bizard, Quebec, the club participates in the world's oldest international interclub match against the Bostonians of The Country Club, Brookline, Mass., the centenary of which was celebrated in 1998.

Charleston, however, seems to be where it all began in America. The first English settlers had arrived at what is now Charles Towne Landing on the Ashley River in 1670, after King Charles II awarded Carolina to the eight English noblemen known as the Lords Proprietors. After the colonists revolted against proprietary rule in 1719, the proprietors' interests were bought out and South Carolina, now a Royal Province, quickly became an attractive site for settlers. This was largely due to its religious tolerance and freedom in addition to its lucrative seafaring trade. When the *Magdalena* arrived, she berthed at the fourth largest city in America.

Charlestonians were strong supporters of their rights as Englishmen in the Stamp Act crisis of 1765, and a year after the Declaration of 1776 it was Henry Laurens, a Charleston merchant who served as President of the Continental Congress. Indeed, the first decisive American victory of the war was the repulse of Commodore Sir Peter Parker and his squadron of nine warships who attacked the fort on Sullivan's Island which protects the seaward entrance to Charleston. The city was thus saved from capture, and the fort was renamed after its gallant commander, Colonel William Moultrie. He was the son of a Scots emigrant physician Dr John Moultrie, whose family estate was on Moultrie's (now Multrees) Hill in Edinburgh.

And in a final delicate twist to the story of golf and Charleston, Multrees Hill is today the site of the Scottish Record Office from where the final search continues for the origin of those first clubs, carried by the good ship *Magdalena* as she sailed into harbour past Sullivan's Island – and brought the greatest game to America.

Golf goes East: India

In the year 1829 golf left home, again. This was to be the last year of the life and reign of King George IV, the jewel in whose imperial crown was India. Scots being prominent in the colonial administration and commerce of Bengal, it was not surprising that the ancient and healthful exercise of their ancestors should engraft here. And thus it came to pass that the first surviving golf club outwith the British Isles was inaugurated on a site at Dum Dum, a north-eastern suburb of Calcutta which was itself capital of the Raj until the move to Delhi in 1912.

The club was initially known as the Dum Dum Golf Club, sharing the name with a particularly nasty type of bullet. However, it was smartly changed to the Calcutta Golf Club when it relocated in the 1880s to the British imperial cantonment, The Maidan, literally 'the open field' in Bengali. The apotheosis to Royal Calcutta took place in 1910 in the aftermath of the Great Durbar when King George V and Queen Mary bestowed their royal patronage. By this time the club had moved again, this time to the splendidly named suburb of Tollygunge to the south of the city centre where, in great state, it reposes to this day.

Tollygunge means 'Tolly's market' and is named after Maj. William Tolly, an English military engineer who in 1775-6 widened and dredged a branch of the Hooghly river, itself a distributary of the Ganges, sacred to Hindus. Known ever after as Tolly's *nullah* or canal, this was a seventeen mile long waterway for people and goods coming in to Calcutta from East Bengal and Assam. Tolly levied a charge upon each and every vessel using the waterway, thus silencing his critics who had christened his project Tolly's Folly. The revenues, known as Tolly's Lolly, made Tolly and his wife Moira, known in Bengal as Tolly's dolly Molly, extremely wealthy and easily able to pay Governor Warren Hastings 60,000 rupees to acquire, as their home, Belvedere House which is now the seat of India's great National Library.

The transposition of golf and golfers to the subcontinent was not without drama. The climate of India is in general far hotter than that of Scotland, where even the wettest wet day in Fort William is a passing shower compared to the thunderous cascading deluge of an Indian monsoon. The vastly complex Indian caste system was also in stark contrast to the British version in which individuals are simply ranked by their category of golf club, ranging from Crazy Golf, Pitch 'n Putt, Municipal, Pay&Play, Private – *Keep Out!*, and so on up to the dizzying pinnacle of the R&A.

But perhaps it was the cuisine that required most acclimatisation. The British digestive system, accustomed as it had been for centuries to a gentle regime of broth, tripe and puddings, was totally unprepared for the assault of curry. In India it had to deal progressively with mild Kormas, moderate Dopiazas, hot Madrasis and hottest of all, the feared King Prawn Vindaloo, a curry whose internal effects measure up to 6.7 on the Richter scale. Indeed the Vindaloo problem doesn't end there, because exactly four hours later comes the terrible reckoning.

Vindaloos and related curries have a temperature just below the melting point of lead and, on discharge, produce a condition known to medical science as AFA (Acute Fulminating Ano-proctitis) better known to the lay public as the Ring of Fire. This led to many early casualties among golfers fresh out from Britain and unaware of the post-Vindaloo perils awaiting them from fire ants, scorpions and king cobras as they fled the fairways into the adjoining jungle and lowered their incendiarised posteriors, literally, into the unknown.

A famous golfing term is also of Indian origin. 'Tiger line' is now used to describe the tightest line one can take when driving at a doglegged hole. It is also the most dangerous line, and not just from the possibility of a lost ball. In 1852, a shaken Lt Rupert 'Tusker' Carrington-Dalby of the 16th Lancers based at Howrah, staggered back to the clubhouse at Dum Dum calling weakly for a *burra peg* – a large whisky. Teeing off at the 4th and trying to cut off a major part of the dogleg, he misheard the warning cry of 'Tiger line, Sahib!' from his caddy Gulbindar Singh. He then pulled his drive into the adjoining jungle where he was confronted by an enraged Royal Bengal tigress and pursued at high speed round and round a tree, then back across the fairway, round and round more trees before finally leaping into a *tankh* (pond) from which he emerged a wetter but wiser man.

This officer, a scion of the Berkshire Carrington-Dalbys and nephew of the then Governor-General of Bengal, Lord William Bentinck, had his first game in India as a guest at Government House. On his return his Lordship summoned Lal Chatterjee his bearer and caddy. 'And how did the young Sahib get on today?' The bearer, displaying that finesse and diplomatic *double entendre* for which Bengalis are justly famous, said 'Oh, the young Sahib played most *divinely*, but God was *very* merciful to the birdies.'

A serious *bon viveur*, the Eton-educated Tusker got into numerous scrapes with authority during his time in India. Tired of writing letters of apology to his hosts and hostesses, he devised and had printed the stiff white card shown below. This he called a General Apology, known to his friends as Tusker's Omnisorry, which his *sirdar* (chief servant) would furtively take round to the scene of his last *débâcle* and shove under the door, before legging it back to camp.

Lt. the Hon. J.R.T. Carrington-Dalby, 16th Lancers,
presents his compliments – and his unreserved apologies
for his outrageous and totally unacceptable behaviour at your:

At Home
Chukka
Tiffin
Wedding   *Kindly tick as appropriate*
Dinner
Tiger Hunt
Bar Mitzvah
RSVP   *Funeral*   *Pour mémoire*

Terrified of the intestinal convulsions which could also be brought on by impure *pannee* (water) he gradually abandoned the stuff altogether and by the time he was a Major in the 4th Rajputana Rifles his intake was, as he himself said, 'a model of consistency'. This was correct. He now drank *only* alcohol. He was once asked by his incredulous Brigadier's wife how he managed it, and for example, what did he use when cleaning his teeth? 'A light Sauterne, Ma'am,' was the classic response.

The establishment of Royal Calcutta Golf Club paved the way, or rather the fairway, for the foundation of other clubs. Royal Bombay came in 1842, Bangalore in 1876 and the Shillong Golf Club ten years later. In Ali Sher, Arjun Atwal and Jeev Milka Singh, Indian golf has produced players of the highest calibre, just as it has produced courses of the highest altitude. Shillong, capital of the Indian state of Meghalaya, is situated at an altitude of 5,000 ft (1,500 m.) above sea level in the foothills of the Himalayas. It is thus a good acclimatisation centre for golfers preparing for an assault on that absolute summit of golfing endurance, Gyamchchona GC.

Situated in high Kashmir, Gyamchchona is the world's highest golf course. It lies at a height of 16,300 feet (4968 m.) on the slopes of Kanchenjunga, the third highest Himalayan peak after K2 and Mt. Everest. The turf, buried under yards of snow for half the year, is soft and good while the greens are fast, being a combination of moss and a variety of high-altitude grasses. However, the sensational feature is of course the thin air, which will permit a full-blooded drive to pass 400 yards in flight.

At Gyamchchona, preparations for a round are, to say the least, unusual. All fourballs, having submitted their intended route and ETR (estimated time of return) must engage Sherpa guides as caddies and then be securely roped together. This at least ensures that all lost balls are hunted for by the whole group, and by the Sherpas who double as stretcher-bearers. Those making it alive to the 5th green, the apex of the course, sing their National Anthem and are then routinely photographed; their country's flag and their clubs making a strange collation with their goggles and oxygen cylinders.

Back at the clubhouse a visitor, asking if anyone had ever hit a ball at a higher altitude, will receive that beatific Indian smile and the assurance:

'Only one, *Sahib*. An American Admiral.'[1]

'Really – and where on earth was that?'

'Why *Sahib*, it was not on Earth, but upon the Moon...'

---

[1] In February 1971, Rear Adm. Alan Shepard USN, commander of Apollo 14, used a Wilson six-iron head fixed to a lunar sample scoop-handle to strike, single-handedly, two golf balls for, he said, 'Miles!'

MIXED FOURSOMES

The mixed foursome, or even the mixed pairing, is by far the sternest test of both golfing and interpersonal relationships. For a man and a woman to leave the 1st tee in a happy, productive and meaningful relationship is not uncommon. Neither is it uncommon for them to return in a state of armed neutrality, or with the storm cones up and flying. The male-female partnership in golf works best at the courtship or even at the fumbling pre-courtship stage for there is nothing like a round of golf to reveal character on both sides. Many a union has been forged, and many sundered between tee and green. In other words, what happens between the shots may be as important as between the sheets.

People vary. Some men relish the thought of a lady life-partner who's a good driver and can make a pitch or smack a 2-iron round a dogleg. In contrast, some will do absolutely anything to avoid developing a romance with a lady who is at all interested in the game. This type wants to play with his mates, go on trips to the Algarve with them, to 'hang' with them as the Cousins say so artistically. He probably belongs to one of the diminishing number of all-male clubs where the facilities for women are cunningly rudimentary and their presence tolerated on well spaced occasions. Such a man may indeed admire a well set up lady with a good setup, a howitzer drive and a smooth approach. He may decide, however, that a smooth approach of his own should be abandoned in favour of a remoter admiration, perhaps delivered though the protective medium of the clubhouse windows.

Women needed courage to take up the game in the early days. As was noted elsewhere in this book the very first two ladies of golf were both queens and victims of outrageously bad behaviour by their husbands. Mary Stuart died by the headsman's axe and Catherine of Aragon perished in Kimbolton Castle while effectively under house arrest. Nothing daunted, ladies were eventually to overcome the most extraordinary array of difficulties placed in their paths to the 1st tee.

First there was the notion that sports were exclusively for the boys. As games were a continuation of, and substitute for, weapons training and preparation for the regular warfare of former times, they were no place for women. No, these frail creatures were best left at home. A woman's place might be on the washing & drying green, but certainly not on the putting variety.

Then the medical argument was wheeled out. Gynaecological textbooks of the nineteenth century advised specialists in training (then all male) that indulging in sports was positively harmful to reproductive capacity. This might result in at best the production of weak and feeble infants, or at worst in infertility. And as women were expected in those days to be either pregnant or lactating, it would be improper for them to compromise their obstetric performances by discharging on the golf course, tennis court or, heaven forfend, the athletic field, the energy required to conceive, incubate and then produce the next generation of Empire builder.

George F. Carnegie was a St Andrean golfer and poet, who favoured the world in 1833 with a poem entitled 'The Golfiad' (a play on Homer's *Iliad*) in which he concisely distributed the activities of the sexes in golf:

The Game is ancient, manly and employs,
In its departments, women, men, and boys:
Men play the game, the boys the clubs convey,
And lovely woman gives the prize away,
When August brings the great, the Medal day!

No doubts about the duties then. Men strike, boys caddy, and while a woman naturally may not lift the prize for herself, she is deemed quite capable of lifting it from the prize table to present to the manly victor.

The first recognised female golf club in the world was not formed until 1867 at St Andrews where for 30 years activities were restricted to Himalayan putting, well away from the gentlemanly games trundling past on the Old Course. But old habits and attitudes live long in clubhouses. As late as 1898 Sir James Moncrieff, a member of the North Berwick club who sat in Scotland's Court of Session as Lord Wellwood, handed down a terrible judgement on women in golf. 'If women' he boomed, 'choose to play at times when the male golfers are feeding or resting, no one can object. At other times, they are in the way.'

So that was it, effectively until the twentieth century. Women were of course useful and indeed necessary for domestic and reproductive activities, but on the golf course they were simply, as his Lordship had clearly indicated, in the way.

No longer. When the new century opened, national women's competitions were already underway and the activities of such tremendous organisers and fixers such as Issette Pearson saw to it that there was no going back. These days, the vast majority of golf clubs have lady members and the mixed foursome competition is a regular on the calendar.

Humour flashes both ways between the locker rooms, the ladies making no secret of their amusement at the men's extraordinary belief that the consumption of a couple of G&Ts, claret with the lunch and a couple of stiff Kummels to wash it down will do no harm to their hand and eye coordination in the afternoon.

Men, on the other hand, finding little to complain about regarding the ladies' presence in the clubhouse, resort to fictional accounts of female standards of play. A male fourball, for example, is said to have paused on the 10th tee one evening to watch an extraordinary performance by a lone member playing the hole behind. A soaring drive was followed by a top. A cracking fairway 3-wood led to a shank into the deep stuff, from which an effortless recovery to 6 feet was followed by a putt 4 feet past. He caught up with the watching fourball.

'Willie, what on earth's going on?' they said. 'A touch of inconsistency creeping in?'

'Not at all, boys. I'm practising for the mixed foursomes on Saturday, but it's Muriel's bridge night, so I'm having to take all her shots myself.'

Women, like men, make golfers of all shades of ability. At the top of the scale one has only to think of Alison Nicholas, nicknamed 'shrimp' for her stature, which is a pole apart from her stature in the game. This is the petite English girl who in 1997 went over to the Witch Hollow Course in Oregon and returned with the Harton Semple trophy as the US Open champion. It was a particular pleasure to assist her with her speeches as Captain of the Solheim Cup team.

There are among men, some who consider themselves (silently if they've any sense) as somehow the stronger and more resilient sex. They should stop reading at this point. A scientific meeting attended by the author at King's College, Cambridge, had been called to consider the anomaly of the male breast, a singularly useless object provided in duplicate to every newborn lad. The meeting reached a startling conclusion. There were not two sexes, but one – and it was not the male. The evolutionary, genetic, anatomical and physiological evidence, taken together, strongly indicate that men are actually highly specialised women! The implications of this for golf club committee structures, handicapping, R&A membership and especially tee-box positions are so momentous that this section of the book had better end now, while its (formerly) male author reaches shakily for a restorative. Suffice it to say that the story of women's golf – and of women in golf – is far from over.

THE STYMIE

I n golf, a stymie was said to exist when an opponent's ball lay on the green in the direct line between your ball and the cup. If his ball was over six inches away from yours it had to be left as it lay. Thwarted from holing out and in a virtually impossible position, you were thus left, if the opponent's action had been deliberate, in a state of powerless and incandescent rage.

The term 'stymie' thus entered the English language to describe any situation where normal progress has been intentionally blocked by an adversary. Attached to it also was more than a whiff of suspicion that the blockage, if not actually illegal, smacked of sharp practice. Thereupon, stymie-rage might rapidly escalate to direct physical action. This was most likely should it transpire that the perpetrator, curiously never called the stymier, though frequently called illegitimate[1] by his stymied victim, was benefiting financially from the manoeuvre. Golf's stymie is in contrast to other sports such as croquet and snooker. Here stymieing also occurs, but the action of snookering or blocking an opponent's shot on the billiard table is perfectly legitimate. In general, however, to find oneself stymied may be defined as being scandalously prevented from getting one's own way by a human, or rather inhuman, agency unable to grasp one's own progressive and selfless agenda.

The golfing stymie was eliminated in a landmark ruling of 1952 when the Rules Committees of the R&A and the USGA, bowing to public and police pressure, removed the blockage and declared the action illegal. Disputes arising from stymies are as old as golf itself, but matters came to a head with the notorious Stymie Duel of 1930 on the practice ground at Royal South Devon GC, which left both parties with gunshot wounds and the Hon. Julian Fitzmaurice on a fast boat to Patagonia.

Much less well known is the origin of the term itself. It derives from Capt. John Davie Stymie (1768 – 1847) of the frigate HMS *Euripides*. Stymie was a man of many talents. A fine classical scholar, he was a translator of the essays of Seneca. He was also the first to properly classify sea urchins and is believed to have been the inventor of the bathing wig. However, at various times in his career he managed to halt Royal Naval operations in peace and war by getting himself – and *Euripides* – into positions of total obstruction. Known in the fleet as a one-man blockade, the gregarious Stymie was nonetheless a great favourite of Admiral Nelson who regularly accepted his explanations that *Euripides* was basically unstable and the very devil to handle upwind. Other captains were heard to observe drily that it was Stymie himself who was basically unstable, the very appearance of an upwind-heading *Euripides* resulting in the rest of the squadron literally getting their anchors, and the wind, up.

---

1 A chap unable to trace his ancestry back to his father.

At the battle of Cape St Vincent in 1797, Stymie and *Euripides* managed to get themselves sandwiched between Capt. Thomas Troubridge's three-decker battleship HMS *Culloden* and the gigantic Spanish flagship *Santissima Trinidad* with which *Culloden* was in furious combat. Having taken a terrible pounding from the broadsides of both (and from Troubridge's loudhailer) *Euripides*, now dismasted, careered off downwind and rammed the Spanish frigate *Mercedes* which promptly sank. This was just as well for Stymie who otherwise would have been heading back upwind for a serious roasting from peppery Sir John Jervis, C-in-C Mediterranean.

Even more spectacular was his performance in 1822 at the Grand Fleet Review by King George IV at Spithead. Here, Stymie completely lost control of *Euripides* which veered towards the sedately approaching royal yacht, the R.Y. *Royal George,* about to receive salutes from the guns of the long line of anchored men-of-war. To avoid a collision, *Royal George* had to change course violently and unexpectedly, depositing His Majesty and his regal entourage on their backsides in the lee scuppers just as three cheers and a chorus of *Rule Britannia* roared out from the flagship. *Euripides* then coasted helplessly along between the royal yacht and the battleships of the Home Fleet, an acutely embarrassed Stymie receiving 21-gun salutes from each ship (and powerful signals from *Royal George*) before mercifully running aground on Gunnery Reef.

Eventually, like the old seadog himself at the end of his career, the stymie came ashore, crossed the beach and slithered ominously on to the golf links. There it lay, obstructive, inflammatory, between the other ball and the hole, immovable – and legal. It was possible to putt round it, but that cost strokes and in all probability, loss of hole. You could chip over it but that resulted in a divot or divots in the centre of the green and enraged greenkeepers. You could of course putt *at* the stymieing ball, but if you hit it your opponent could then, without penalty, either play it from the new position or replace it. Worse, if you hit it and thereby knocked it into the hole, your opponent was deemed to have holed out. Or you could concede defeat, pick up your ball, hand the stymie ball to its smirking owner and head grimly for the next tee.

There were of course two types of stymie: one broadly acceptable; one potentially lethal. The first type was the fortuitous stymie, usually regarded by both parties as a Rub of the Green and just as likely to happen to one party as the other. Totally different, however, was the act of 'laying a stymie' where a player putted his ball deliberately into a position to deny his opponent the chance of holing out. This tactic was usually off-limits in matchplay games between old friends and in club competitions. However, when the match was between two personal foes with an old festering sore or score to settle or, even better, between two countries such as England and Scotland, well now, that was different! In the latter case, with a thousand-year history of cross-border raiding, arson, cattle rustling and indiscriminate homicide, a well laid stymie could and would ignite the blue touchpaper in no uncertain fashion.

Such was the background, then, to the famous final in the Borders Cup of 1908 between the English Royal Northumberland Golf Club from Newcastle-upon-Tyne and the Scots of the Melrose Reivers Golf Club. It was played, as it is to this day, over the Cheviot course which actually straddles the Border. The match points were poised at 5 – 5 when the final singles game was seen approaching the 18th green. Matters were clearly tense and the body language of both parties seen to be clearly combative as word came up to the watchers at the clubhouse that the match lay all square.

What follows is a reconstruction of the events on the final green which was attested by both parties after leaving hospital. Playing for the English club, Edward Percy's good drive lay slightly shorter than that of Robert Douglas of Melrose. Playing first, Percy then hit a superb soaring approach to the centre of the green, the ball rolling up to no more than six feet from the pin. Douglas also hit the green but was a further eight feet away. At this point the dialogue between the two players requires to be set out. Percy, a scion of the ducal family of Northumberland had an accent that would make Prince Charles sound like a welder, while Douglas sounded just like the burly Selkirk hill farmer that he was.

Coming on to the 18th green and with the match on a knife edge, it was perhaps not surprising that the long simmering historical card was played. Thus:

Percy: 'Of course these encounters are hardly new. For centuries you Douglases were all involved in, shall one say, the cross-border livestock transportation industry. All through the Middle Ages you chaps would come down our way, armed to the teeth, and with the sole purpose of running off the sheep and cattle'.

Douglas: 'Aye, we did. I'll no deny it. We did gae hame wi' selections frae yer herds an' flocks. But ye must understaund, Percy, that was nae the prime objective',

Douglas putts – 3 feet short and left.

Percy: 'Really. So what, pray, was the prime intention?'

Percy putts – 1 foot short and in line.

Douglas: 'We came for yer women.'

Percy: 'Really?'

Douglas putts – Stymie!

Douglas: 'Aye, it was only when we *saw* yer women that we went hame wi' the sheep and the cattle'.

A grim and brief handshake followed, to cheers from the watching Scots contingent.

Percy: 'Well, thank you for the game, Douglas, and also for confirming what has been a long held suspicion in my family'.

Douglas: 'And whit might that be?'

Percy: 'That no Scotchman will hesitate when given the choice between a woman – and a *sheep*'.

THE COMING OF THE OPEN

In September 1859 Allan Robertson, aged only 43, died at St Andrews. In his day without question the finest golfer in Scotland, he was also a feathery ball maker and both employer and playing partner of the then young Tom Morris. Robertson, known as 'The Laird of the Links' had been, literally, one of the driving forces of the game. But now he was gone, and a question arose. Upon whom should the mantle fall as the finest player in the country? Some averred that it must be Morris, now Keeper of the Green at Prestwick, with whom Allan had differed over his assistant's adoption of the newer gutta-percha ball in place of the lucrative but fragile feathery. Many, however, said no, the greatest player now is clearly Willie Park of Musselburgh. At this the clamour grew that Andrew Strath of St Andrews deserved consideration, as did Robert 'the Rook' Andrew of Perth, Charlie Hunter of Prestwick St Nicholas and George Daniel Brown, down in London at the Blackheath Club. The issue clearly required settlement. Came the hour – came the man. Enter the father of The Open, Major James Ogilvy Fairlie of Coodham.

Fairlie, joint founder of Prestwick GC in 1851, was a remarkable man: soldier, landowner, sportsman, Captain of the R&A in 1850 and already a championship innovator. In July 1857 he had been the driving force behind a 'Grand National Golf Club Tournament', the first ever national club competition. This was a foursomes matchplay event held at St Andrews under the auspices of the R&A and won by the Blackheath Club from London. The competitors having all been gentlemen amateurs, it then occurred to Fairlie and his friends that a national competition, in strokeplay rather than matchplay format, might be held to determine the champion professional.

It should be remembered that in the mid-Victorian era, professionals as we know them today did not exist. The landed gentry who belonged to the great clubs had been adding to their staffs of huntsmen, jockeys and gillies the new phenomenon of the caddy *cum* playing partner who would evolve into the modern professional golfer. Such were Allan Robertson and Tom Morris who until 1859 had both been an integral part of the running of the St Andrews amateur tournaments. But now Robertson was dead and the newly proposed tournament would at least go part way to ranking the professionals. It would also place the crown – or buckle on the belt as it turned out – on the 'Champion Golfer of the Year' a title still applied each July to whoever hoists and kisses the Claret Jug.

In May 1860, the Prestwick Golf Club minutes begin to speak about the organisation of the first Open Championship. The prize was to be a decorated red morocco belt costing £25, the equivalent of £1,100 today. It would be retained by the Club or (on deposition of a bond) by the winner for a year. Should a winner repeat his victory in the two succeeding years, the belt would be his to keep. The similarities with the belts awarded to boxers are unmistakable, this being the era when gentlemen might have prize-fighters in their employ for the big money, bare-knuckle contests much patronised by the landed gentry.

And so it came to pass that a decree went out from Lord Colville, Prestwick's Captain, to the clubs of the golfing world that 'known & respectable *Cadies*' (sic) might enter a competition to be held on Wednesday, 17 October 1860. This was during the week of Prestwick's Autumn Meeting, at which the competitors would also caddy for members, a useful financial incentive since there was no prize money to accompany the belt. Caddying during the Meeting would also allow the outsiders to get a feel for the layout of the great and unique Prestwick links.

Directly across the town's Main Street from the cottage of Tom and Agnes Morris, there sits to this day the Red Lion Hotel, then a preferred watering hole of the Ayrshire Yeomanry Regiment of which Maj. Fairlie and other Prestwick members were officers. Indeed it had been following a Yeomanry Field Day nine years previously, on 2 July 1851, that there assembled at the Red Lion a group of fifty-seven local professional men and gentry headed by Fairlie, then Captain of the R&A. They proceeded to inaugurate the first links course of the west of Scotland, electing as first Captain, Archibald William, 13th Earl of Eglinton and Winton and head of the great Ayrshire family of Montgomerie. The noble Earl, in return for granting leave to the Glasgow & South Western Railway to cross his estates, had extracted the right to command any train carrying him to stop and either uplift or deposit him, anywhere. He was thus ensured of door-to-door delivery of himself, his playing partners and entourage from Eglinton Castle to a convenient hundred yards from Prestwick's original 1st tee.

The competitors were instructed to assemble before the Red Lion Inn on that very first morning of The Open. They were eight in number, the longest journey being G.D. Brown's from London, the shortest Tom Morris's who had only to cross the road. The tournament would consist of three rounds of the then 12-hole Prestwick links beginning at noon. The first two rounds would be followed by a mid-afternoon lunch back at the Red Lion and then a final afternoon round. It is just as well that slow play was then unknown, since sunset at Prestwick on the 14th of October falls at just after a quarter past five, by which time three rounds had to be completed.[1]

No effort was spared to police the matches with appropriate rigour. The Rules of the Prestwick Club were read to the competitors by the umpire, Sir Robert Hay of Hay Lodge and the pairings, each with their Marker, were announced. The 39-year-old Morris would lead off with Robert Andrew (Perth) accompanied by their marker, Andrew Gillon Esq., of Wallhouse. They would be followed by:

Willie Park Sr. (Musselburgh) & Alex Smith (Bruntsfield) *Marker*: Capt. James.

Wm. Steel (Bruntsfield) & Charlie Hunter (Prestwick St Nicholas) *Marker*: Capt. Pratt.

George Brown (Blackheath) & Andrew Strath (St Andrews) *Marker*: Maj. Fairlie.

---

1 Sunset was at 17.16 hrs GMT. British Summer Time (Mar – Oct) was not inaugurated until 1916.

Willie Park went straight into a three-stroke lead after the first round and held on to it at lunch. The final afternoon round saw Morris catch up one shot, but the championship and the Belt went to Musselburgh. Park finished on 174 – or 6 under 5s – two strokes ahead of Morris, Prestwick's Keeper of the Green and six ahead of Andrew Strath. The *Ayrshire Advertiser* reported:

' *…the most veteran frequenters of the Links will admit that in all their experience of Morris, they never saw him come to grief so often, because it is well known that the battle of Bunker's Hill is an engagement which he has very seldom to fight.*'

From this we may surmise that it was in sand, laid by himself in Prestwick's bunkers, that Tom Morris's challenge had perished, the reporter's allusion being to the first great battle of the American War of Independence on Boston's Bunker Hill some eighty-five years previously. Who caddied for Morris is not recorded in his written account of the day, held in the Prestwick Club's archives. Sadly, the truancy records for the Autumn Term of 1860 at the neighbouring great school, Ayr Academy, have not survived to tell us if a certain 10-year-old pupil, one Thomas Morris Jr., was unaccountably absent from class that day…

It will be noted that, strictly speaking, the first Open was a rather closed affair. Professionals only had competed and Maj. Fairlie moved quickly to propose that Prestwick Golf Club should, literally, open the 1861 competition to include gentlemen amateurs. The advertisement stated that the Tournament was now 'Open to the whole world'. It worked. There was a 50 per cent increase in the field – to twelve – which included Fairlie himself. The belt then returned from East Lothian to Ayrshire with Tom Morris winning the first of his four Open Championships. Fairlie led the gentlemen players and was thus the first ever Leading Amateur. That title remains a great honour to this day, the presentation ceremony of The Open beginning each year with the award of the Silver Medal to his latest successor.

Thus began the first and still the greatest of the Major championships. The number of rounds has increased to four and the prize fund to a value beyond the conception of those first eight competitors. However, to this day The Open remains a strokeplay competition open to amateurs as well as professionals and is always held upon a great Scottish or English seaside links course over four tremendous days of high Summer. And there is not a small boy standing today with a club in his hand and a ball at his feet who does not dream of having his name engraved upon that old Claret Jug and standing in succession to where Willie Park of Musselburgh stood with James Ogilvy Fairlie of Coodham all those years ago, on a windy Autumn day of fitful sunshine, upon the links of Prestwick.

THE LAWS

The Rules of Golf are earthbound and are determined, codified and enforced by the R&A and the USGA. The Laws of the game, however, are determined by forces poorly understood by science – which question and sometimes violate gravity and levity, logic, metaphysics and even the 2nd Law of Thermodynamics.

These forces come from the zone *beyond* the twilight zone, where the fabric of space-time is curved like a boomerang hook by the 'dark energy' of Einstein and shot throughout with mysterious dark matter. It is the scatter of this latter matter that holds the Universe in thrall, the stars in their courses and the golfball in flight. Down at the quantum level, the forces allow an object, unlike Hamlet, both to be and not to be *and*, if in being, to be in two places at once – like your bandit opponent's ball.

The Laws, pregnant with meaning, also groan with symbolic and semiotic import. In this they resemble America's symbol of the nation, the magnificent bald eagle (*Haliaeetus leucocephalus*) a bird now so freighted with analogy and so weighted with symbolism as to have the greatest difficulty in leaving the ground.

Seek not to uncover that which is concealed. Accept the precepts ordained by the Laws and go down boldly to the clubhouse in the pre-dawn darkness. When the rosy-fingered dawn streams in the firmament, stand in good order and smite the dimpled one until the mantling night brings close of play – and renewal to the ragged trouser leg of care.

Here, then, are the known Laws. Of those which are as yet unknown and whereof we consequently may not speak, it is, as the (later) Wittgenstein posited, advisable to remain absolutely mum:

The ball flies best when struck with the Practice Swing.

Perfect shots may finish in imperfect places.

The ball visible far ahead in the rough is not a ball at all – and if it is, it is that of your opponent.

Concedable[1] putt lengths contract in inverse proportion to an opponent's lead, ego – and especially house size.

The caddy's cry that the missing ball is actually below your foot will come just after you have *stood* on it – thereby violating Rule 18 and incurring loss of time, temper, hole – and caddy.

Finishing at the 17th – or starting at the 2nd – reduces gross scores by a minimum of six.

No ball flies straighter and truer than The Wrong Ball.

A new putter will not work until reduced to cowering obedience by being (a) bent over the knee *and* (b) whacked against a hardwood tree *and* (c) taken to the Range to have its flight characteristics thoroughly explored.

The rhythm of a downswing in progress cannot be improved by mentally rehearsing the Duckworth-Lewis method, or the line-ups for the 1949 World Series. However, mentally rehearsing Duckworth-Lewis[2] or the Yankee / Dodgers '49 line-ups[3] during the *backswing* will materially improve rhythm, direction and distance.

On the tee, when tortured by uncertainty as to whether one's drive is, or is not, OB – it is. Tip: *If uncertain, throw a* provisional *tantrum and / or club.*

In match play, loss of a hole through three-putting will inevitably lead to loss of the ensuing hole to a birdie on handicap.

---

1   Known, curiously, as a gimme (sic) in the US.

2   A fiendishly complex method of calculating what a cricket team's score *would* have been in a 50 over match, had play not been abandoned due to rain after they had faced only one over – and made 1 run, the other team having scored 350. Useful in conjunction with the English summer.

3   The Yankees won in five games, finishing under the lights of Ebbets Field and starting an unbeaten run of five consecutive World Series wins. The Duckworth-Lewis method is not used in baseball – yet.

Pythagoras' Theorem[4] originally stated:

τηε ηειγητ οφ ανψ τρεε λψινγ διρεχτλψ βετωεεν βαλλ ανδ γρεεν ισ εθυαλ το, ορ γρεατερ τηαν, τηε απεξ οφ τηε σηοτ ρεθυιρεδ το χαρρψ τηε λενγτη οφ τηε ηψποτενυσε)

(*Translation:* The height of any tree lying directly between ball and green is equal to, or greater than, the apex of the shot required to carry the length of the hypotenuse.)

An approach played after an inordinate wait for the green ahead to clear will be topped. Furthermore, it will travel a distance inversely proportional to the time spent waiting.

The only persons capable of (a) understanding the Macroeconomic Cycle (b) clearing the National Debt and (c) running the Country, work as caddies or cabbies.

Character is determined by a player's attitude to – and treatment of – a divot which has had the gall to outdistance the ball. All divots receive gentle, loving replacement after glorious floated approaches to 3 feet.

However how bad it is, it can – and will – get worse.
However good an opponent is, he can – and will – improve... *unless:*
Tip: *Tell him you've never, ever, seen him play so well.*[5]

A golf club's character is determined by (a) the greens (b) the showers and (c) the port; the golfer's character by the sequence in which he enquires of these facilities.

Butterflies can and will commence a distracting racket in the adjoining meadow, starting as you go dormy 4-down.[6]

The easiest putts are curved thirty-footers for triple bogey.

Coincidences on the golf course are never coincidences. e.g.:
Player: Why, that's my wife up ahead – playing with my *mistress!*
Partner: Odd coincidence, that...

---

4   Pythagoras of Samos (fl. sixth century BC) Ancient Greek polymath, philosopher and clearly, golfer. Drew his geometric propositions and theorems in the dust with a stick, i.e. a Scratch man.

5   This technique is called Regression to the Mean – the opponent automatically worsens in order to balance his earlier birdies, restore the Order of the Universe etc. Nettled opponents have been known to describe it as an aggression *of* the mean.

6   First described in *The Clicking of Cuthbert* (1922) by P.G. Wodehouse. Young Mitchell Holmes missed short putts due to the uproar of butterflies in the adjoining meadow.

A ball still missing in rough after a nine minute search will be found exactly 25 yards further back.

The only available replacement for an absentee from your regular friends' fourball is the reigning Club Bore.

It is inadvisable to hang by the neck while waiting for a bandit to self-penalise for a Rule breakage.

Shanks arrive like the Piccadilly omnibus on a pouring wet day; none for ages, then three back to back.

When playing with the President or the Prime Minister – or preferably both – fear not when your drive lands behind a tree. At your approach, the 'tree' will sidle away.

The formula for calculating the velocity (Vds) of a player's downswing is;

$$Vds = Sbs \times Hc$$

i.e. Speed of Backswing (Sbs) multiplied by Handicap (Hc)
Thus: Backswing 20 mph; Handicap 15.0; Downswing = 300 mph.

The Driver's Licence of lady professionals entitles them to: (a) take it slowly back (b) pause at the top for 10 minutes and then (c) hit it 290. In contrast, male amateurs do not pause *at* the top, bring it down at 290 – and then have 10 minutes to find it.

British Golf Club Dinners shall abandon the 10-minute midway *Interval, Comfort Break, Ease Springs* or other euphemistic claptrap.

Replacing it from the Rules of Golf shall be: *Rule 25; 1 (b)*[7]

Playing Into an Irish gale, three good shots will be required to get on in two.

---

[7]   This R&A / USGA Rule provides for golfers requiring relief – from accumulations of casual water...

The difference between a golfball and a clean handkerchief – is that a man will spend ten minutes looking for a golfball.

If, seen from afar, one ball is on the edge and the other is in the bunker, your ball is in the bunker. If, on closer approach, the ball on the edge permits no stance, your opponent's ball is in the bunker. When both balls are in the bunker, yours is in the footprint made by a Sasquatch.

It is easier to get up at 6:00am to play golf, than at 10:00am to watch *Face the Press,* or to perform any household chore.

The Lightning Warning horn is programmed to sound just as you go to 3-under, or 3 up, whichever is the greater.

Scorecard pencils have real power, including the ability to deprive bookies, investment bankers, even Professors of mathematics, of the ability to count above six...

A Scottish caddy will never, in his entirre *life*, have seen a wurrrse shot than *that*.

THE R&A

On Tuesday, the 14th day of May in the year of grace 1754, twenty two 'Noblemen & Gentlemen' who almost without exception belonged to the Fife aristocracy or landed gentry, convened at St Andrews. They resolved, nem. con.[1] that there be established a Golf Club. It would be entitled the Society of St Andrews Golfers and its green, or golf course, would be the linksland bordering the great bay which sweeps round from the town towards the estuary of the river Eden. The founding fathers were;

The Rt Hon. Charles, 5th Earl of Elgin and Kincardine

The Rt Hon. James, 5th Earl of Wemyss

The Hon. Thomas Leslie

The Hon. James Leslie

The Hon. Francis Charteris

Sir James Wemyss, Bt

Sir Robert Henderson, Bt

Lieut.-General James St. Clair

David Scott of Scotstarvit

James Oswald of Dunnikier

Prof. David Young, Univ. of St Andrews

James Lumsdaine Esq., Provost of St Andrews

James Wemyss of Wemyss Hall

Walter Wemyss of Lathockar

John Bethune of Blebo

Henry Bethune of Clatto

Thomas Spens the Younger of Lathallan

James Cheape of Sauchie

Arthur Martin of Milntoun

Maurice Trent of Pitcullo

Robert Douglas, Esq.

Prof. John Young, Univ. of St Andrews

Almost exactly 250 years later, in May 2004 the R&A celebrated its great birthday with a series of golfing and social celebrations which are indelible in the memories of all who took part in them. The last formal dinner was The International, held beside the first fairway of the Old Course in the great marquee which was on two floors and held 1,300 individuals from all over the golfing world. That evening, the author of this book had the pleasure of proposing the toast to 'The Club & Game' to which the Captain, HRH the Duke of York, replied.

---

1 *Lat.* Nemine contradicente: unanimously. Lit. 'No-one speaking against'.

What follows is an extract of these remarks, the full text having been lodged with the R&A Secretariat. This is in the hope that *they* may be of some use to the proposer of the same Toast at the Tercentenary in 2054 since the author, at the age of 108, may have to reluctantly give way to a younger man.

TOAST: THE CLUB & GAME

In the *highly* unlikely event that I were ever to eagle the 17th on The Old, the mighty *Road Hole* of St Andrews, the pleasure would be small compared to that of receiving from Charles Philip the letter of invitation to speak tonight on the occasion of the R&A's great birthday – and to speak also of the great game, known to our stern ancestors here in Scotland as The Ancyent and Healthfulle Exercyse of the Golff. This game I have loved since I was but a boy on the links of Prestwick St Nicholas with a club in my hand and a ball at my feet and, as the great Irish poet Yeats said for all our childhoods: 'when I was young – and never a crack in my heart'.

It was in the reign of the Captain's royal ancestor King George II, that those twenty-two noblemen and gentlemen inaugurated their Golf Club in the town which Andrew Lang, that great classical scholar and friend of Robert Louis Stevenson, was to celebrate. These wistful lines were written in his rooms at Balliol College, Oxford, a century and a half ago.

St Andrews – by the Northern Sea
A haunted town it is to me!
The grey North Ocean girds it round;
And o'er the rocks, and up the bay
The long sea-rollers surge and sound;
And still the thin and biting spray
Drives down the melancholy street...

The list of the R&A's founders begins with Charles, 5th Earl of Elgin, chieftain of the ancient family of Bruce and descendant of Scotland's greatest monarch, King Robert I – Robert the Bruce. It was in his fourteenth century reign that our long War of Independence closed with the Treaty of Edinburgh, ending with the pen what had begun with the sword. And it was perhaps in that very reign that, with peace – came a game.

Eighty years later, in 1834, the title *Royal & Ancient* was applied to the Club by command of our Sailor King, William IV, and in 1854, the centenary year of its foundation, the famous clubhouse was opened. By the late nineteenth century, the R&A had assumed responsibility for the Rules of Golf and it now of course administers the game worldwide, with the honourable exception of the United States and Mexico which are under the aegis of the USGA, whose President has graced these celebrations.

But the game – the game was old when the R&A was young. Whereas we know precisely when those gentlemen at St Andrews struck their agreement to found the Club, we do not know – and indeed we can never know – when the first club struck the first ball on a links in Scotland. What is certain, however, is that the game known to us as the Golf is old – and old beyond the memory of Man. One has only to stand late in an evening by the 18th green here, or at Prestwick, or at Sunningdale or Pine Valley or at your own home course as the twilight, the 'gloaming' as we call it here, slowly deepens and enfolds the links, to feel the presence of those who went before us. They who long since have played their last rounds and left us, in the Golf, a priceless legacy. As our old poem runs:

Ane by ane they gang awa'
The Gatherer gathers great and sma'
And ane by ane - maks ane and a'.

Those were the men who conceived this game and who brought it to birth. They then nurtured it, codified it – and took it away with them on their wanderings and emigrations throughout the known world. And on many a foreign field and links and heathland, golf was to take root and flourish and become an ornament to the lives of the peoples who adopted it.

Had Scotland given nothing else to the world; if you took away all our discoveries, inventions and advances in the physical and natural sciences, in engineering and in medicine; if you subtracted all that vast achievement and had it *only* been the Golf – then I say we could still hold up our heads among the nations. For I believe it to be a truly civilising game, encompassing as it does respect for opponents, courage in adversity – that greatest of the virtues as Churchill reminded us – and an acceptance, *with good grace*, of the victory, or the defeat, which Dame Fortune hands down.

Thus we have today an ancient game of which we in our golf clubs and our homelands are the modern custodians, and also a set of Rules – both written and unwritten – of which the R&A and the USGA are the jealous guards.

I look forward to each edition of the Decisions of the Rules Committee not only for its illustrative judgements, but also because of the sheer opulence of the English language in which they are couched. And have you noticed the marvellous contrast between the language of the Question put to the R&A and the language of the R&A's Answer? For in the question you can actually *smell* the cordite – you can hear the thunder of disputation, you can sense the acrimony over a Rules issue so stubborn that it has had to be tied up, hauled to St Andrews, and hurled to the ground before the R&A for settlement.

And then, in response, cometh the *Answer*. Like a flooding tide it comes, euphonious and grandiloquent, irresistibly sweeping away ambiguity and error, replacing bile with balm and spleen with equity and sweet reason. It sounds exactly like a decision of the Supreme Court – which of course is exactly what it is. However, within the mellifluous language, the R&A still contrives, just occasionally, to convey the merest hint of irritation that the Question might have been, well, more precisely *formulated...* Thus, from Australia:

Q: Is a snyke an outside ygency?
R&A: A *live* snake is an outside agency; a *dead* snake is a loose impediment.

Nor does the R&A forget the young. It invests heavily in providing instruction to the children of all ages who are the very life of the game to come. This is epitomised by a splendid Notice by the first tee of the short children's course at Gullane in East Lothian. It reads, sternly, *Adults may only play on this golf course - if accompanied by a child.*

Golf, the great teacher, also imparts to the young the Golden Rule, itself a great lesson for life in this uncertain world. This is the lesson that you have no prospect of mastery over the game, over the golf course, or over the opposition unless – or until – you are first master of yourself.

This was never better put than by Sir Henry Newbolt in his famous poem with its Latin title of *Vitai Lampada* – the Torch of Life – a poem that many of us will recall from our own schooldays. In the last verse we find:

> *For this is what our sons must hear,*
> *And none that hear it must forget.*
> *This they all, with a joyful heart,*
> *Must bear through Life like a torch in flame,*
> *And falling, fling to the host behind,*
> *Play up, play up, and play The Game...*

And so, I put to this great company the incontestable proposition that both Club and Game are worthy of a toast. A toast, then, to the R&A, our generous hosts tonight who are also our enlightened legislature and our wise judiciary.

A toast also, to the Game itself. A Game like no other. As fine a field Game as any ever conceived by the mind of Man:

The Ancient – and healthful – Exercise of The Golf.

Pray rise...

EARLY CLUBS AND SOCIETIES

The Society of Edinburgh Golfers*	1735
The Gentlemen Golfers of Leith	1744
The Society of St Andrews Golfers	1754
Bruntsfield Links Golfing Society	1761
Blackheath, London	1766
Musselburgh	1774
Aberdeen	1780
Crail	1786
Glasgow Gailes	1787
Cruden Bay	1791
Dunbar	1794
Glasgow Golf Club	1797
Montrose	1810
Scotscraig	1817
Manchester	1819
Leven	1820
Perth	1824
North Berwick	1832

Traditional. The Society's Minutes date from 1773.

EARLY CLUBS WORLDWIDE

INDIA – Royal Calcutta	1842
FRANCE – Pau (first golf club on the Continent)	1856
AUSTRALIA – Royal Adelaide	1870
NEW ZEALAND – Dunedin Golf Club, Otago	1871
CANADA – Royal Montreal	1873
SOUTH AFRICA – Royal Cape	1885
USA – St Andrews Golf Club, Yonkers, NY	1888
ARGENTINA – St Andres	1892
CHINA – Shanghai	1896
HONG KONG – Hong Kong	1899
JAPAN – Kobe, Mount Rokko	1901
ITALY – Circolo Roma, Acquasanta	1903
SWEDEN – Hovås, Gothenburg	1904
SPAIN – Madrid Polo Club	1914
ICELAND – Reykjavik	1934

The Apple Tree Gang
– and the Great C.B.

The town of Dunfermline, the Scottish nation's ancient capital, is situated in the Kingdom of Fife and holds a remarkable place in the history – of the USA. It was the birthplace of the industrialist and philanthropist Andrew Carnegie in 1835 but by far its most important export to America was not one individual but two gentlemen who were to establish, over there, one of the greatest conceptions of the Scottish mind and the subtitle of this book; *The Ancyent & Healthfulle Exercyse of the Golff*. Now, there may be reports of Dutchmen playing kolf in Fort Orange[1] in the 1650s and of clubs and balls being exported to the Carolinas in the 1740s, but when it comes to the formal establishment of a Golf Club, the place is Yonkers in the State of New York. For there it was, on 14 November 1888, that the St Andrew's Golf Club[2] inaugurated club golf in the Land of the Free. The parents of this lusty and fast-growing infant were the two men of Dunfermline: John Reid, the club's first president and Robert Lockart, supported by their friends Messrs. H.O. Tallmadge, Harry Holbrook and John B. Upham.

Lockart, a linen buyer, was home in Scotland in 1887 when, at the St Andrews of no apostrophe, he acquired from Old Tom Morris's shop the set of clubs and gutta percha balls with which he and John Reid effectively launched the US game. The most famous of their several early venues was a 15-hectare orchard at Yonkers, NY where, to paraphrase the Israelites of old, they hanged their coats upon the apple trees and smiled when they thought of Zion. Hence the term 'The Apple Tree Gang' for the founders of this great club. Future members were to include the air ace Eddie Rickenbacker who had shot down twenty-six German aircraft over the Western Front; the great architect Stanford White, himself sensationally shot down at Madison Square Garden by a jealous husband; and another son of Dunfermline who had gone west and done rather well in America, the aforementioned Andrew Carnegie.

The St Andrew's Golf Club relocated in 1897 to Hastings-on-Hudson and to this day maintains contact with Scotland's and indeed the world's oldest club, the Royal Burgess Golfing Society of Edinburgh (Est. 1735) which is thus forty-one years older than the United States itself. Both clubs continue the traditional eighteenth century uniform of the Red Jacket, effectively a traffic light imposed on golfers by the Town Council of Edinburgh (after several serious injuries) in order to halt citizens from straying into the paths of fast-flying featheries on the urban links of Bruntsfield and of Leith.

---

1 Now Albany, NY.
2 Note the apostrophe, inserted to avoid any conceivable confusion with the 'Home of Golf'.

In 1871, some 16 years before Lockart's visit to Old Tom Morris at St Andrews, that grand old man had taken under his wing a 16-year-old student who was to become the powerhouse of golf's conquest of America. This was Charles Blair Macdonald, known to all and sundry as CB, who had been sent by his wealthy Chicagoan parents to study at St Andrews University in the homeland of his grandfather. Here he majored in golf, joined the R&A and competed with and against 'Young Tom' Morris, then thrice Open Champion. CB returned to the States with the firm intention of engrafting the game of his ancestors on to the sporting life of his homeland. A man of iron will and seismic personality, Macdonald and some associates inaugurated, in 1892, the first 18-hole course in America for the Chicago Golf Club at Wheaton, Illinois.

In September 1894, CB entered the 'U.S. National Amateur Championship' hosted by the Newport, Rhode Island Golf Club, where William G. Lawrence had the effrontery to actually beat CB (188 to 189) over 36 holes of strokeplay. Never a man to come second in anything, Macdonald promptly challenged the right of the competition to call itself 'National' though not before entering another 'National Amateur Championship' this time at the St Andrew's Golf Club. However, after lunching on champagne and steak with Stanford White he *again* came second, this time to Laurence B. Stoddard. This was clearly intolerable as CB knew in his heart and soul that *he* was the best amateur in America. By sheer force of personality he had the aforesaid championships effectively annulled by promoting, with H.O. Tallmadge of the St Andrew's Golf Club, the inauguration of a truly National Body, which would then hold a truly National Event which he, the truly greatest player in the nation would surely and finally, *win!*

And so it came to pass that a meeting was held in the Calumet Club in New York City on 22 December 1894. Here, his own Chicago Club together with those of St Andrew's, Newport, Shinnecock Hills and The Country Club at Brookline, Mass., became the charter clubs of the Amateur Golf Association of the United States, later retitled the United States Golf Association. The following year, the first official US Amateur Championship was held at the Newport Country Club ending with a 36-hole Final. In this match and by the still unmatched margin of 12 and 11, CB achieved his apotheosis, walloping the hapless Charles E. Sands into that horrid, unacceptable second place from which he, Charles B. Macdonald, Amateur Champion of the United States, indeed of the New World, now emerged in majesty.

Macdonald was also a pioneering golf course architect, a term he himself invented. He has such great courses as Mid-Ocean, Bermuda and Yale to his credit, together with his masterpiece, the National Golf Links of America near his home at Southampton on Long Island. Here he incorporated many of the classic features of British courses such as the Redan at North Berwick[3] and the Alps at Prestwick[4]. Fittingly, it was over this course in 1922 that there were played the inaugural Walker Cup matches between the USA and Great Britain & Ireland.

---

3   The 4th at the National and the 15th at North Berwick. A Par 3.

4   The 3rd at the National and the 17th at Prestwick. A par 4 requiring a blind approach shot.

C.B. Macdonald made one final contribution to transatlantic golf, namely the harmony in which the game has developed on both sides of the great water hazard. Whereas, in the US the other two great British field games of rugby and cricket both underwent major metamorphoses, into football and baseball respectively, golf was to remain on parallel tracks in both nations and indeed everywhere. To this day, one of the strengths of world golf is the collaboration over equipment, standards and especially the Rules of Golf between its two governing bodies, the USGA and the R&A. This was largely due to CB's membership of the R&A's Rules of Golf Committee for a period of more than twenty years, while being simultaneously the Rules guru of the USGA. Although independent bodies, they have worked particularly closely together since 1952 (when the stymie was declared O.B.) to produce a uniform rule code, so that the same laws apply wherever the game is played. Americans may drive to the course on the wrong side of the road and wear suspenders[5] and knickers[6] on the links but, by jove, they play it as it lies.

And so the amateur game literally took off in America. There were only eighty courses in the U.S. in 1896. By 1930 there were nearly 6,000 with nearly triple that number today. But the sheer strength in depth of US golf is perhaps best seen in the US Amateur Championship itself. In 1898, three years after CB took the inaugural title, the Havermeyer Trophy went to Findlay Douglas of St Andrews. However, for her next US champion, Royal Aberdeen's Richie Ramsay, Scotland would have to wait no less than one hundred and eight long years… The Americans had arrived.

5   Braces.

6   Plus Fours. (Short for Knickerbockers).

GOLF IN IRELAND

When the game first crossed the Irish Sea from Scotland to the Isle of Emerald is unknown, but once it got there it stayed and Erin is now the home of some of the finest courses in Europe. The Scoti, the Gaelic-speaking Irish tribe who gave their name to the Scots, had crossed the sea in the other direction in the sixth century AD, bringing with them a truly remarkable Celtic stick and ball game. This was the lightning-fast organised mayhem known to this day as hurling in Ireland and as *camanachd* or shinty in Scotland. It is not a relative of golf by definition, as it involves a moving ball struck at by the players of both teams, each wielding a single stick. This is known in both countries as a *camán* and thus hurling and shinty are much more akin to the modern game of hockey. However, golf in Scotland may actually have begun when a lone *camanachd* player, all others on the field having been incapacitated, began to strike the ball, or *sliothar*, towards a target or hole in the turf. Indeed, only a few modifications are necessary to turn a hurling stick with its curved tip into a golf club and a hurler into a golfer. There is another parallel with golf: just as the Dutch called their own game kolf from *kolven* their word for clubs, so the Gaelic *camanachd* derives from the *camán*, the playstick.

Golf in Ireland is a unique experience. This is the island of Erin, the land of saints and scholars where, during the Dark Ages from the sixth to the tenth century, the torch of learning survived and flourished when all was chaos over continental Europe. Ireland may be a modern state of Europe, but it is also an ancient and unique state of mind. Thus golfing visitors to the country are well advised to be prepared, since here the unexpected is an everyday occurrence; and the impossible by no means unknown.

The Irish have a wondrous facility with the vocabulary, grammar and syntax of the English language which partly derives from the silver of their own native tongue. This is the ancient language known popularly as 'The Irish' or 'The Gaelic', and whose correct title in linguistics is Erse. Being non-Germanic in origin it is in short, very different from English. For example the affirmative 'yes' and the negative 'no' are, in Irish Gaelic, virtually unknown. If you say to an Irishman: 'Sir, are you Seumas Cormac O'Malley?' then if he is, he will say proudly, 'I *am*, surely!' Ask him, however, if he is Seumas *Dermot* O'Malley and he will say, 'Surely I am no such t'ing!'.

Erse also contrasts dramatically with the Romance languages which are derived from Latin. A famous example is Prof. Brendan Kennelly's response to a Spanish visitor to Trinity College, Dublin, who wanted the Gaelic word for the state of mind and inaction known in Iberia as *mañana*. Ah, well now, said the great man, there were several words that were close – but none that quite managed to convey, well, the same sense of *urgency*.

In the Gaelic, the sometimes spectacular divergence between the spelling of a word and its actual sound can also be a trial for the uninitiated. For example, Dublin's port of Dun Laoghaire manages to be pronounced Dunleery. This produced a splendid Limerick, a verse form which is itself an Irish gift to literature;

There was a cute man from Dun Laoghaire
Who propounded an interestin' theoghaire
That the language of Erse,
Has a shortage of verse,
Since the spellin' makes poets so – weoghaire...

Indeed the very term of Erse for the original language can itself cause confusion. Some years ago I was External Assessor to an appointment board at UCG – University College, Galway. We were charged with the appointment to one of the Chairs of the medical school, at a time when it was required that all Professors display at least some facility with the Irish language, i.e. the Erse.

The Board being convened for the interviews, the Dean said: 'Now, gentlemen, we will proceed to assess the academic, scientific and clinical attributes of each of the four candidates; and when we've finished, each will be taken next door to have his Erse examined.' At this, there was a visible start from the other external assessor, an English academic of great renown. Clearly unaware of the linguistic import of the Dean's remark, he said to me, *sotto voce*: 'Did he say what I think he said – about the candidates having their – you know – *examined*?'

I said that this was indeed so. 'My God,' said he, 'they are *thorough* over here...' Some time later the successful candidate was brought back in to be congratulated, his Erse having passed with flying colours. I could then set off for Scotland, naturally via Dublin, and the great course of Portmarnock.

This peerless links was the venue where on one occasion the SUGS[1] team arrived to find a young but fast-growing Irish hurricane blowing over the golf course, while at regular intervals sleet showers hurled themselves at the clubhouse windows. I stood doubtfully at the porch with the Irish captain and an old caddy I'd known for years, wondering if we could actually go out in the wild conditions.

'What do you think, Dermot?' said I to the caddy. Back came the classic response;

'Jasus, doctor,' said he, 'sure the rain's bad enough, but is it not the fierce wind? T'twoud... 'twould blow a tinker off his missus!'

It's the unexpected which is the joy of the place. A carload of English golfers had become hopelessly lost on the maze of backroads around the great links course of Lahinch in the County Clare. At last, help appeared to be at hand. An Irish agriculturist was leaning over a roadside gate. They stopped. Down went he passenger's window;

---

1 The Scottish Universities Golfing Society (Est. 1906). Another splendid body of men.

'Good morning, Sir.'

'Mornin'

'I say, how do you get to Lahinch?'

(pause)

'Mostly, me brother takes me.'

Ask a straight question – get a straight answer. And the same goes for Detective Chief Supt. James P. Murphy of the *Garda Síochána*, the Irish police force, who led the hunt for the stallion Shergar, the Aga Khan's 1981 Derby winner who had vanished from his stud at Ballymany, Co. Kildare.

Some of this officer's statements at his press conferences have gone rightly into journalistic legend. 'Our problem,' he said at an early conference, 'is that, well, we just don't have a clue.' Now, he meant 'clue' in the old policing sense of a lead, but the alarm bells began to ring at HQ in Dublin. With the international press now present in force, an American journalist rose at the next press conference to say that he understood that the heist had actually been carried out by six guys, but in Supt Murphy's opinion, who was *behind* them. 'Who's behind them?' he said, 'Well, quite obviously, we are!' But with the trail growing ever colder and no sign of the horse, he gave a final splendid estimate of poor Shergar's whereabouts. 'Either the horse is out of the country now,' he said decisively, 'or else, he's still somewhere in Ireland.'

Erin produces great players. Over to England in 1947 for The Open Championship at Hoylake came Fred Daly of the Balmoral Club in Belfast. A week later, the first Irishman to win it was on his way home with the Claret Jug, having said in his acceptance speech that, sure, the venerable trophy would now benefit from a change of air! A change of air is what Ireland gives the arriving golfer – and the change begins when you're still *in* the air, especially if it's an Irish airliner.

'Captain O'Shea speaking' came the voice from the cockpit as the flight from Edinburgh carrying our visiting fourball arced high over the Irish Sea in the general direction of Ballybunion. 'We're now cruisin' at twenty eight thousand feet over the Isle of Man and we'll shortly commence our descent – to arrive at Dublin International Airport in precisely – in, er, approximately… one moment please *(pause)* Ah, sure in no time at all!'

And so, from the oldest golf course in Ireland at The Curragh in Co. Kildare, up to the superb natural links of Ballyliffin in Co. Donegal and over to Royal Co. Down in Northern Ireland, a golfing feast awaits. This should be washed down of course with a glass or two of the famous black wine of Ireland as the evening sun sinks into the Atlantic, only to rise over the largest nation ever to press the greatest game firmly to its heart – America.

COLONEL BOGEY

Major Frederick Joseph Ricketts[1] RM was a golfer and a Royal Marines bandmaster who composed one of the most famous military marching tunes of all time, the 'Colonel Bogey March'. One legend has it that the eponymous colonel was a character who played at Ricketts' own golf club, while another has it that Ricketts, based at Plymouth in Devon, picked up the idea while a guest at the United Services Golf Club[2], near the Royal Navy base at Portsmouth in Hampshire. This club had followed the lead of Hugh Rotherham of Coventry Golf Club who, in 1890 had standardised the number of shots that an idealised good golfer would take at each hole. This was originally termed the 'ground score'. This concept permitted match play games to be conducted not just against an actual physical opponent, but also against a mythical figure who would unerringly shoot the ideal score for each hole. The idea had spread to the links of the Great Yarmouth & Caister Club where a member was heard to complain to the Secretary, Dr Tom Browne, RN, a former naval surgeon, that this peerless golfer – as yet unnamed – was the very devil to beat, a veritable 'bogey man'. This term came from a popular music hall tune of the time sung by Val Rosing, then resident singer with Henry Hall and his Orchestra. On their gramophone record (78 rpm) of the smash hit song 'The Teddy Bears' Picnic'[3] the flipside track was:

Hush! Hush! Hush!
Here comes the bogey man!
Don't let him get too close to you,
He'll catch you if he can!

The name itself derives from the old Scots word 'bogle', a terrifying phantom or spectre. Indeed in Robert Burns's great narrative poem *Tam O'Shanter* the tipsy hero, riding erratically home from a tavern in Ayr after a market day in 1791 is described as, 'glowrin' round wi' prudent cares, Lest *bogles* catch him unawares'.

Tam was right to be cautious. Shortly after careering past what is now Belleisle golf course in a storm of wind and rain, he and his long suffering grey mare Meg hear music. They then stumble on a dance of witches and bogles in full swing in the ruined Alloway Kirk with, on bagpipes, none other than Satan himself. After shouting at a comely young witch who is wearing a very short shift, or 'cutty sark,' Tam has to ride for his life for the bridge over the nearby river Doon, pursued by the screeching harpies and bogeymen. He barely gallops to safety over the bridge (witches of course being unable to cross running water) although in the process Meg loses her tail to the pursuers. And that is why the world's most famous clipper ship the *Cutty Sark* has as her figurehead a beautiful witch in her cutty sark, holding in her left hand – the grey mare's tail.

---

1   He composed under the pseudonym of Malcolm Alford.
2   Now the Gosport & Stokes Bay Golf Club.
3   It sold 50,000 in the first week.

The term 'bogle' crossed the Atlantic, mutated to 'booger' and reappeared in Henry Hathaway's *True Grit*, one of the best Westerns ever made. In one of the dialogues between Marshal Rooster Cogburn (John Wayne) and young Mattie Ross (Kim Darby) we hear;

Rooster: You scared of the dark?

Mattie: I've *never* been scared of the dark.

Rooster: Well if I had a pistol like that, I wouldn't be scared of no *booger man.*

Mattie: I'm *not* scared of no *booger man!*

So it was at Great Yarmouth that there emerged the notion of the *golfing* bogey man, or Mr Bogey, who would catch you out every time your score failed to match his perfect prowess on the links. He would, literally, catch you if he could. Thus it was that from the original concept of the 'ground score' and from the musical score of a hit children's song, there gradually emerged the bogey score.

But how did he acquire his military rank? Enter once again Capt. Browne from Great Yarmouth on a visit to the United Services Golf Club (USGC) at Alverstoke in Hampshire whose hon. sec., Capt. Seely Vidal of the Royal Engineers had just worked out the 'ground score' of the course. At this critical juncture, in came Capt. Browne with his concept of the mythical Mr Bogey. They reckoned without the military mind. A *Mister* Bogey at the USGC? Outrageous! This Bogey chap was clearly a civilian and thus totally unacceptable at a club where all members were officers of the Army, Navy or Marines. If he's that good and worthy of being saluted, said Vidal, then let's promote the fellow to a decent rank – say, full Colonel.

Thus was Bogey commissioned and began his imperial march across the linksland of the British Isles. And perhaps it was here at the United Services Club that Major Ricketts the golfing Marine bandmaster, incidentally Britain's equivalent of America's great John Philip Sousa, was to discover him and set his march to music. To this day, many clubs still hold Bogey competitions when the first question put to a returning member calling weakly for a large brandy will be, 'So, Willie, I see you lost to the Colonel!'

As befits a soldier, Colonel Bogey was later to go to war. Although famously adapted by Malcolm Arnold for the film *Bridge on the River Kwai*, the tune with its catchy two opening notes (a falling third) saw active service in every theatre of operations.

Indeed its propaganda value was incalculable in poking fun at the physical and alleged reproductive deficiencies of the Nazi leadership. All over the old empire the Colonel fell in beside Tommy Atkins and his comrades in the Allied infantry – and as they marched they sang;

Hitler, has only got-one-Ball!
Goering, has two, but ve-ry small,
Himmler, has something sim'lar,
But poor old Goebbels, has no Balls – *at aaall!*

The golfing term of bogey has now evolved to mean a score of one over par which is itself an interesting term, brought to golf not by the military but by the uniformed civilians of the Stock Exchange – but that is another story. Meanwhile the Colonel's deathless ghost, still a worthy opponent, marches across the fairways to Major Ricketts' peerless tune, recalling faint yet powerful memories of golf in our great grandfathers' time – and of campaigns long ago.

DR. STABLEFORD

My much esteemed and late medical colleague Dr. Frank Stableford (1870 – 1959) was a member of the Royal Liverpool Club whose course is the great championship links of Hoylake. More relevant to the present account, however, is that he had been since 1914 a member of Wallasey Golf Club which is also on Merseyside. For it was to be from here on 16 May 1932 that, having entered its final form, the deeply humanitarian points-scoring system which bears his name was launched across the golf courses of the world.

Concerned at the mental and physical trauma caused in strokeplay competitions where a single disaster at any hole, especially the first, could wipe out the round, he conceived the notion of a points award at each hole. This contained two strokes of genius. The first was that, after holing out, you went to the next tee – and started again! A disaster at the previous hole would apply to that hole only, not to the entire round. The other stroke of genius was his idea that points would cease at an absolute upper stroke limit, finally set at two over par. At or above this it was, literally, pointless to continue and you were free to scoop up your ball and stamp off to the next tee. This had the dual advantages of maintaining interest in the game and of speeding up play. There being no stroke indexing at that time, Dr. Stableford's method was initially played off scratch with points calculated points against Colonel Bogey, thus:

1 over Bogey – 1 pt. 2 over – 0 pts.

Bogey – 2 points.

1 under Bogey – 3 pts. 2 under – 4 pts.

The initial format had been proposed not in England but over the border in Wales where Frank Stableford, a military surgeon, had been a member of the Glamorganshire Golf Club prior to his mobilisation and departure for South Africa and the Boer War. *The South Wales Daily News* of 30 September 1898 reported the results of the Autumn Meeting at the Club, giving the first ever public notice of the new system. Note that, following the custom of the time, the player is imagined to be actually playing against the Colonel.

'Each competitor plays against bogey, level. If the hole is lost by one stroke only, the player scores one; if it is halved, the player scores two; if it is won by one stroke, the player scores three; and if by two strokes, the player scores four. To the total score thus made, one third of the player's medal handicap is added.'

Apparently Frank Stableford didn't play in the Autumn Meeting which began his experiment and which, interestingly, had a handicap limit of fifteen. However, according to the Glamorganshire Club, he donated a special prize to the winner, a Mr. W. Hastings Watson, who had returned a commendable forty-two points, a sporting gesture typical of the man.

Over thirty years later and now at Wallasey, Frank Stableford who was now over 60, revised the system to allow the full handicap to be added, rather than one-third. A further refinement came when a series of strong gales, with consequent high scoring, revealed that the system was favouring the higher handicap players. It was then decided that the handicap allowance should be taken selectively at the more difficult holes, instead of simply adding the full handicap allowance to the points scored. The welcome advent of the Stroke Index (SI) can be assigned to a meeting of the Council of the National Golf Unions at York in 1924, after which the stroke indexing of holes could be recruited to determine, hole by hole, the points to be awarded. Usually 7/8ths of the player's handicap is allowed, although many competitions simply award the full handicap. The advent of par rather than bogey as the datum point or benchmark was the final refinement and the Stableford Points system entered competitive golf as a boon and a blessing to those of us who are recurrent visitors to gorse bushes, beaches and O.B. territory in general.

The Vale of Glamorgan shares with the Wirral Peninsula the honour of being joint midwives to the birth of the Stableford System. A portrait of the man hangs in the Glamorganshire Club at Penarth near Cardiff, as does one at Wallasey and it's entirely fitting that a Stableford match was inaugurated between the two clubs in commemoration of their joint places in golfing history.

Professional golf has, very occasionally, run tournaments based on a modified Stableford system. The International tournament at Castle Rock, Colorado, in 2002 was one such on the PGA Tour. It was won by Rich Beem with a 4-round aggregate of 44 Points which is roughly 22 under par. Clearly inspired by Dr Stableford, Beem went on to win a Major the very next week.[1] However, the pros clearly prefer the 4-round standard stroke play format against all alternatives including matchplay.

The modified system awarded points as follows:

Albatross (Double Eagle in the U.S.): 8 pts.

Eagle: 5 pts. Birdie: 2 pts.

Par: 0 pts.

Bogey: minus 1 pt. Double bogey or worse: minus 3 pts.

This format is deliberately skewed from that used in amateur competitions. This is to encourage players to go for eagles and birdies which carry rewards much greater than the penalties incurred for par or worse. Holes-in-one carry no extra points, an ace at a par-3 being scored simply as an eagle.

---

1   The PGA Championship, at Hazeltine National GC with a score of 278. He held off Woods.

In 1959, his medical colleagues had to tell the 88-year-old Dr. Stableford that his progressive loss of vision was untreatable and would shortly end in total blindness. Life without sight and without his beloved ball games of golf and snooker was not acceptable to him and he ended his life with a pistol in his own study. He lies in Frankby cemetery, in the Wirral.

The Wallasey Club where in 1930 Bobby Jones qualified for his Grand Slam Open down the road at Hoylake, remembers the good doctor with the warmest affection. He was elected Captain in 1933, the year after his system was inaugurated and was made a Life Member twenty years later. There is a plaque to his memory on the golf course and it is sited, thoughtfully, by the 2nd tee. This is perhaps because the tragedy of having a disaster at the first hole in a Medal or other strokeplay competition crystallised his final idea of a system of points. Since 1969, the Frank Stableford Memorial Open, naturally using his system, has been held there every Spring on the anniversary of that long ago May morning when his great contribution to the game emerged from its chrysalis in its final format.

He served his country well as a military surgeon first in the Boer War and then in the First World War, when he was a major in the Royal Army Medical Corps. He was a fine doctor in the care of his patients, just as he was a fine captain of his club. A scratch golfer, he had a gloriously colourful personality with his bright bow ties and yellow Rolls Royce. But it was his service to his fellow men and women that we cherish most. We remember the humanity of the simple System by which Dr. Frank Barney Gorton Stableford will himself ever be remembered by every club golfer and by every errant driver. Let the last word be said by that splendid golf writer and BBC commentator Henry Longhurst:

'I doubt whether any single man did more to increase the pleasure of the more humble club golfer.'

Absolutely correct.

Dermot F. Mulligan

In contrast to the celebrated Dr Stableford whose biography is well researched, there has hitherto been a veil of uncertainty surrounding the origin of The Mulligan, the retaken drive. Indeed it was only with the release this year in Galway of the family papers of the late Dermot Mulligan that the story has begun to come to light.

Dermot Fingal Mulligan was a respected horse breeder and dealer from the vicinity of Ballinasloe, Co. Galway in the west of Ireland. He came of an old Republican family and was a witty and gregarious man with a wide circle of friends in the equestrian community of Erin. Many of these he would entertain at his stud near Ballydangan during the famous Ballinasloe Horse Fair, held on the town's Fair Green in the first week of October. This is perhaps the greatest such event in Europe, attended by some 80,000 world authorities on horseflesh who descend annually on this bustling market town on the River Suck.[1]

Mr. Mulligan was also a golfer and a prominent member of the Correenbeg Golf Club, known locally as the golf & hurling club. The latter title referred not to any Gaelic game activity, but to the propensity of exasperated members to fling errant clubs into the Suck, flowing peacefully beside its narrow fairways. Indeed the interesting American expression, 'This thing *sucks*!' indicating displeasure, derives from Correenbeg emigrants along the Hudson describing an item worthy only of discharge into it.

Now, Dermot Mulligan had a physical problem. It was of great rarity, unsusceptible of cure and of fascination to the general public. It has been the subject of several learned articles in *The Lancet* and of many more in the less academic *Sun* and *News of the World*. It is neither an infection nor an allergy nor a malignancy. It flares up episodically and without warning causing its victims embarrassment without limit and sometimes injury. Like its neurological cousin the Gilles de la Tourette syndrome[2], in which the patient suddenly shouts imprecations without obvious provocation, Mulligan's disability was an autonomous and capricious entity. And, unlike Tourette's, his problem was not up in his head, it was down, well down, below. Dermot Mulligan had progressive anorectal stenosis (PAS) which is also known as de Laval Syndrome after the Swedish scientist whose nozzle principle it illustrates[3].

PAS, as its name implies, is a condition of the rectum or terminal bowel. For reasons not yet elucidated, it becomes progressively narrowed or *stenosed*, leading to a spectacular increase in the speed of gases passing along it. In most cases, classed as PAS Type I, this is not a major issue. It can be detected by barium studies and corrected surgically. However, in the rarer but more serious PAS Type II, as in Mulligan's case, the rectal narrowing is further exacerbated by bowel spasm induced by the gas hydrogen sulphide (H_2S). The spasm narrows the rectum even further, thus accelerating the already fast-passing gas, or wind, to extremely high velocities.

---

1   The Suck (sic) is the principal tributary of the Shannon. A beautiful river, it forms the boundary between Roscommon and Galway for part of its fifty mile journey.

2   Dr.Georges Gilles de la Tourette (1859 – 1904), Parisian physician.

3   Gustaf de Laval (1845 – 1913), Swedish engineer and inventor of the de Laval nozzle which accelerates turbine gases to high Mach numbers.

In these circumstances, it can be seen that the speed (Ve) of gases emerging from the rectum will be given by the equation;

$$V_e = \sqrt{\frac{T\,R}{M} \cdot \frac{2\,k}{k-1} \cdot \left[1 - (P_e/P)^{(k-1)/k}\right]}$$

The actual velocity of emergent wind can reach up to 250 mph and effectively turns the terminal bowel into what is known in aviation as a ramjet. The patient receives only the briefest warning, when a premonitory colicky spasm indicates that the colonic ramjet is about to operate. He knows then to hold on tight to any available structure, since he is about to be powerfully subjected to Newton's Third Law of Motion[4]. Depending on the precise direction in which his rear is pointing when the ramjet goes off, the patient is instantly propelled forwards for up to eight feet if standing, or one foot upwards if recumbent. The volume of expelled gas being relatively small, the episode is not malodorous, while the noise it creates – a thin, high pitched scream – is usually drowned by the even higher-pitched yell of the victim and the alarmed cries of those toward whom he is suddenly and rapidly projected.

Not surprisingly, those afflicted by PAS Type II go to great lengths to avoid dietary items that generate colonic hydrogen sulphide. The precise labelling of foodstuffs in recent years has greatly reduced the incidence of attacks and consequently the injuries caused both to the patient and to innocent bystanders. No diet, however, is perfect. Some foods remain unlabelled and intelligent men like Dermot Mulligan have to take precautions. In former times this was not possible and historians have speculated that certain incidents in recorded history may be explicable in terms of the disorder. Noting that circumstances of high emotion provoke bowel activity, they have postulated that if a person with PAS Type II were, for example, to find himself acutely frightened while carrying a load of colonic H2S, the results could literally, be explosive.

For example, in the ninth century AD the remarkable behaviour of King Egfrith of Northumbria on sighting a Viking fleet off Jarrow from his warship is described thus in Latin by the chronicler Oswiulf of York:

...tandem in puppem regem adligavere quia in mare seriatim propulsus erat.
'Eventually they lashed the King to the poop, since he had been repeatedly hurled into the sea.'

Scholars puzzled over this passage for centuries. No longer. While a fast approaching Viking squadron would give anyone a degree of intestinal anxiety, it would seem that on this occasion PAS Type II, compounded by some dodgy eggs from the galley, had given Egfrith a series of right royal ramjets. He was to get another, courtesy of Erik 'Bloodaxe' Sigurdsson, later in the day...

---

4   Sir Isaac Newton (1643 – 1727) English physicist and mathematician.
    His Third Law states that for every action there is an equal and opposite reaction. It is the principle that powers the jet engine.

Now, you can probably see where this is leading. Dermot Mulligan took great care with both his diet and his bodily positioning in order to minimise an attack. In bed he wore a crash helmet and slept prone rather than supine, the bedstead reinforced by multiple cushions nailed to the headboard. He descended staircases backwards, talking the while and keeping pace with those descending conventionally. Nevertheless, there were casualties, including his own equestrian career. This ended in the show jumping final at the Dublin Horse Show when he was unfortunate to experience a major ramjet just as he and his mare Doonbeg were approaching take-off at the High Wall. It was not Doonbeg but Dermot who took off, incurring a record 28 faults and pithy comments from the wall reconstruction squad. And then there was his golf.

His friends and regular playing partners at Correenbeg GC knew that tension fuelled the ramjet and that Dermot was at his most tense on the first tee. After several incidents when he had rocketed forwards into one of them in the act of making a stroke, they agreed that he would face away until his turn to drive. This was all very well, but his own drive would not infrequently trigger an attack with the ball ending up OB and Mulligan in the gorse bushes. A Local Rule had to be enacted whereby any player distracted, cannoned, or otherwise jetted into by Dermot Mulligan might retake their drive without penalty. This dispensation naturally became known as a Mulligan and rapidly spread worldwide as the generic term for a free reload. At Correenbeg itself, the famous 3M (Mulligan Memorial Matchplay) competition, held at the close of the Ballinasloe Fair, still dispenses with handicaps. Instead, when his opponent is on the backswing a competitor may, without warning, shout 'Mulligan!' a number of times equal to three-quarters of the handicap difference.

Other clubs visited by Mulligan during his lifetime were rather less accommodating and following a spasm at The Open at Carnoustie when he jetted into Juan Gonzalez who was putting on the 17th, he was politely asked by the R&A to restrict his activities to the tented village. Here, however, he was for years the life and soul of the splendid Bollinger Tent.

'Sure, and 'twas no hardship at all, now', said the ever cheerful Dermot later, 'and doesn't good champagne douse the pilot light on the gas!'

THE SECRETARY

My and variable are the duties of the Secretary of your Golf Club and many and heavy the crosses he or she has to bear. Even the name of the office is not inviolate, with many clubs now adopting the title of general manager or chief executive for the person charged with holding it all together. The secretary has to sail serenely above the heaving maelstrom of club politics, dispensing sound policy and imperturbable good humour to all corners of the course and clubhouse. This has to be done while dealing with such major problems as members, visitors, staff and, above all, that colossus which now rules and riles the world, The Healthy & Safe Executive.

Assembled below, from a range of clubs, are some illustrative items from secretaries' correspondence which will demonstrate the sheer mind-bending complexity of the task – and why a good Secretary is not only a treasure, but is to be treasured.

THE HEALTHY AND SAFE EXECUTIVE

Ross Court
Northwark Bridge
London NE1 9HS

Dear Mr. Secretary,

I am writing to you, among a number of golf club secretaries, to seek your views on proposed Directive CPT/4536/10 which is now in draft form before the Executive. As you will know, every year there occur a number of regrettable incidents where caddies have been struck, stunned, poleaxed or indeed flattened by flying golf balls. Enhanced protection would thus seem to be required.

Tests carried out by the Executive's research division on the Army missile ranges on Salisbury Plain have shown that golf balls hit with a driver may reach a velocity of 180 mph or 264 ft/sec. Using retired caddies as targets, it has been found that for protection against significant injury, some form of body armour will be necessary. These tests were carried out using 'Steel Willy' a British modification of the USGA's 'Iron Byron' golf ball driving apparatus, as approved by the R&A's Balls & Implements Committee. It was first established that the traditional caddy dress of raincoat, corduroy trousers and flat cap were no protection from the balls fired by Steel Willy. Indeed, the sight of ex-caddies slowly sinking to the ground after a direct hit was highly moving.

It was then found by repeated trial and error that a caddy standing sixty feet away from Steel Willy would absorb, without injury, a direct hit on the forehead if wearing the MoD's new Mark IV Army steel helmet, and on the solar plexus or the male 'lower abdomen' if clad in a Kevlar armoured vest with pelvic extension. I should emphasise that no caddies died in these tests, volunteers being recompensed, and in some cases revived, with cash and whisky in the standard manner.

The Executive appreciates that the sight of helmeted and armoured caddies may attract a degree of adverse comment. Additionally, since the new MoD headgear strongly resembles the old wartime German Wehrmacht helmet, some of your most senior members may experience a powerful and alarming sense of *deja vu*. I should add that these draft proposals have the support of the politburo of the Caddies and Allied Operatives Union.

The Executive would be grateful if the Club would be agreeable to acting as a test bed for these exciting and progressive innovations and looks forward to hearing positively from you.

Yours sincerely,

John B. Blasdale (Development Executive)

INTERNAL MEMO

From *Captain*
To *Secretary*

Do please give me a report on the state of play with the R&A's new Anti-Doping Drive presently being conducted at the Club. I know you told us something about it at the last Council meeting but some of the members are pretty irate at the activities of the Dopesquad. Old Percy Forbes-Stanford tells me that recently in the Gents lavatory a person wearing a Day-Glo orange suit with a hooded visor, lumbered up behind him with a container while he was having a pee. Having collected a large sample, Mr. Day-Glo then insisted on giving half of it to Percy in a thermos flask-like thing, surrounded by ice. As you can imagine, it was no easy matter for him to convince the others that he'd just been accosted in the Gents by a spaceman and forced to pee in a flask.

Also, I've learned that out on the course yesterday, two other Day-Glo suited creatures appeared, demanding samples from Archie Cruikshank and his playing partners while they were *actually putting* on the 14th green. Apparently when you have to provide a specimen, it has to be there and then and no buts. You can imagine the scene. Just as well there were no ladies about.

Finally, I've just had a phone call from a petrified Angela Gratwick, Henry's wife, to say that yet another Day-Glo is at this moment sitting in her conservatory waiting for Henry to arrive home so that he can blow in a bag. I know we have to help the R&A – but where is it all going to end?

By Friday, please.

Captain.

Mr Secretary *(by email)*

My floribunda (*Stephanotis floribunda*) has produced a deep black mottling on its leaves for the second year now, despite treatment with pentaoxygenated xanthone. I'm in despair. What do you suggest?

H. Farrer

Mr Farrer,

I suggest you stop writing to me with these ridiculous questions. Did someone put you up to this? I repeat for the *n*th time that I know absolutely nothing about Floribundas, or Clematis or anything else that grows, or refuses to grow, in your domestic plot. I am not your gardener; I am your golf club Secretary. So why don't you rip out your Floribunda, mottled leaves and all, drag it to Broadcasting House and shove it in front of the BBC during *Gardeners Question Time*? Goodbye.

2490 Ocean Drive
Tallahootee, Tenn. 38189. USA

Dear Sir Secretary,

Me and 7 other guys of the Tallahootee Golf & Country Club are scheduled to visit England this Fall and we guessed we'd best write ahead to say we'd sure like to include Pinedown in the itinerary. We'd need 4 buggies or 8 live caddies for the day, and we've a real special reason for wanting to say Hi there!

One of us, Harry Pohl Jr who's 85 right now, was a bombardier in a B-17 heavy bomber back in WWII and based at Marley Fen near you. He says that that string of bunkers down the left side of your 17th was done in 1944 by him jettisoning his bomb load one day when they couldn't get the landing gear down! He says he damn near hit the Clubhouse!! Is October 22nd as OK with you for us as it is with us for you?

Sincerely,
Fred J. Yancey

Dear Mr Yancey,

I fear it is not. We do not, as a rule, entertain requests from individuals who begin sentences with a pronoun. Furthermore, the so-called 'buggy' is banned here. This, Sir, is a golf club where one walks the courses.

One can of course sympathise with the desire of Mr. Pohl's crew to jettison their bomb load prior to a crash-landing. However, one has to ask why it has taken over 60 years for the United States Air Force finally to admit responsibility for rebunkering our 17th and, I may say, for the injury to old Perkins. He was struck in the backside by a steel bomb splinter while throwing himself into a gorse bush as your friend roared overhead shedding high explosive. That splinter remained lodged in his person throughout his 55 years here and was the cause of many embarrassing shouted exchanges with visiting Americans, to whom he would insist on demonstrating the wound.

However, we remain allies and if you re-contact this Office enclosing an unreserved apology from a responsible officer at the Pentagon to Mr Reginald Perkins c/o myself, the matter will be reconsidered.

Yours sincerely,

Richard Enwright
Secretary

FROM THE SUGGESTION BOOK

Mr Secretary: Something really must be done about the new vacuum thunderboxes in the Gentlemen's facilities. Lord Portfield, seated about his business, was again sucked down into one last week and had to be extricated, or rather extracted, by myself and Williams. The beast's control knobs are sited behind one's behind and thus, for arthritic senior Members, it is easy to mistakenly depress the "Vacuum" knob when one is desperately seeking "Flush".

Secondly, the "Emergency Vacuum Reverse" function is far too violent. Today, Lord Portfield pressed this knob in error and this time was catapulted right across the khazi, bringing down the hatstand, and Williams, in the process. I suspect you will be hearing at length from his Lordship as soon as he is discharged.

R. J. W. Hogarth.

THE CAPTAIN

It's a tough job, but someone has to take it, head-on. Consequently, the observations below may be of interest to you personally since the captaincy of your club and hence the responsibility for the welfare of hundreds of men, women and juniors both on and off the course may have been, or be about to be, landed upon you.

It's a relentless exposure. The Captain is not only the leader, but is also expected to be omnipresent, omniscient and physically in the lead, the 'point man' as the Cousins[1] say. This point point is literally true. The Captain's every move is followed by a forest of narrowed eyes, furrowed brows – and pointing fingers. As E. Boober Hatch's 'Golfers' Rubaiyat' has it, with usual pinpoint accuracy:

The moving finger points
And having marked, moves on.
Of all thy protests, not a whit
shall haul it down or make it point elsewhere,
for thou, my Captain, are the point of it...

Golf clubs vary in the duties expected of the Captain. In some he is regally non-executive, like the Queen, his duties being to represent the club both at home and abroad, receive visiting dignitaries, control the AGM and so on. However, in most clubs he is, like the US President, a front-line executive. He chairs the living nightmare of the General Purposes Committee, desperately holding the reins of its eight or so member stallions. They, yoked unequally together, pull furiously in varying directions while the club coach thunders along behind swaying perilously, occasionally shedding baggage and threatening to overturn with every change of course, especially when it's the course itself which is being changed.

This difference between the two management styles was perhaps most aptly put by that great judge of Law and men Lord Hugh Griffiths, the only man alive to have been both Captain of the R&A and President of the MCC[2]. A great wit and raconteur, his Lordship once mused on the subject during a speech to a Nags Dinner[3] in the old In & Out Club in London. The President of the MCC, he said, was the boss and what the boss said, in a word, went. In contrast, the R&A were far too smart to let the Captain have *anything* to do with the running of world golf[4]. The Captain might attend meetings of committees but on *no* account was he to open his mouth.

---

1   The Americans. So described in Le Carré's books on espionage. Derived from the play 'Our American Cousin' by Tom Taylor.
    On 14 April 1865, During Act III, in Ford's Theatre, Washington DC, John Wilkes Booth fatally wounded President Lincoln.

2   The Marylebone Cricket Club. Formerly the regulating body of world cricket; owner & operator of Lord's in London, which is to cricket what
    St Andrews is to golf. To a Cousin, the ultimate 'Cruel & Unusual Punishment' i.e. torture, is to be tied up and forced to watch the 24-hour Cricket Channel.

3   The Newspapers' & Advertisers' Golfing Society. A splendid body of men.

4   With, of course, the USGA. *Pace*, dear Cousins.

It is for each club to define the role of the Captain, for he is the club's servant, not its master and he had better believe it, because at each club an average of eight hundred right index fingers are primed, ready to point, should he become too big for his golf shoes. The Captain must be a man for all seasons and in all seasons. He must exude both seriousness and jollity, there being times for him to be seriously jolly and times to be jolly serious. He must be able to reward with a nod, quell with a look and command silence by simply rising, discord being known to abate at the very sound of his voice.

In summary, he must have sufficient qualities of leadership plus a dose of animal magnetism, to allow him to rule his fractious charges by the sheer incompatibility of disorder with his presence. Even when *in absentia*, he must be in command. When the Council of Royal St Lukes were on the point of agreeing to a motion of which the absent Captain was known to disapprove, the Secretary would silently lay the *Taillifer*, the Captain's ceremonial driver, on the table with its head pointing at the proposer of the motion, whereupon that motion would gradually subside and quietly steal away.

The procedure for election of the Captain and the central committee, which we shall call The Council, is a matter of mystery to many members of clubs. Things are at their most confidential in respect of the Captaincy of the R&A, but it is widely believed that there is a pow-wow over an excellent luncheon at the Savoy, involving all past Captains who retain the power of speech. After a Name has emerged and achieved consensus, the proposed new Captain is rung up there and then by the R&A's solicitor to enquire if he fancies the prospect. A persistent rumour in the golfing world (almost certainly apocryphal) is that, some years ago, the Name protested repeatedly that he couldn't *possibly* take it on. The solicitor patiently assured him of admin. support, travelling expenses etc. – whereupon the Name interrupted to ask if it wasn't a precondition of the Captaincy that he be actually a *member* of the R&A? Pause. Click. And back to the drawing board, or rather the drawing room.

In contrast, the Council of Royal St Lukes is chosen by lottery. All the cards of members over the age of 70 and with at least 25 years service are collected. They are then placed in the Waterloo Drum, captured from the French during the battle by Lt. Ponsonby of the 27th Foot and a club member. The drum is then rolled up the clubhouse stairs to the third floor landing, thus shuffling the cards. It is opened and the cards are then cascaded out into the high stairwell by Sgt. Maj. Watkins, the Gate Guardian. Those which land on the second and first floors are eliminated, while those fluttering all the way down and alighting on the ground floor constitute the Council. The card shower is a sight of considerable beauty. It will also be noted that this procedure replicates the method of Degree Assignment, involving marked examination scripts, used by the Deans of Oxford and Cambridge colleges to determine those who are to receive Firsts and upper & lower Seconds.

That night in their Chamber, the new Council elects the Captain. For over two centuries this has been done by the spinning magnum method. The bottle used is one of Kümmel presented to the Club by Peter the Great, Tsar of all the Russias, who visited and played there while in England to study the art of shipbuilding[5]. On the outgoing Captain's command, Sgt. Maj. Watkins spins the bottle in the centre of the Chamber, whereupon all the lights are extinguished. Council members then have approximately 30 seconds in absolute darkness to take up a position which can be anywhere, but must be at ground level. Wall climbing, curtain hanging and piggybacking to escape selection are prohibited. When the bottle comes to rest, the tremendous Tibetan Gong is struck and the lights go up. He at whom the bottle points falls to his knees and is saluted by Council as the new Captain.

After a short night's rest comes the dawn and the ceremony of the Riding In. This is analogous to the R&A's much more recent practice of Driving In at their Autumn Meeting. The new Captain of St. Lukes, dressed in Jacobean costume, rides slowly up the drive on a hopefully docile nag supplied by one of the hunting members.

At the clubhouse doors, watched by Council and a vast crowd of members, he scatters golden guineas for the diving caddies and is handed the ancient play-club *Taillifer*, the symbol of his office. He then rises in the stirrups, brandishes the club aloft and shouts the ancient imperial Roman war cry '*Nil carborundum illegitimi!*' before spurring away to the eastward and the rising sun, as the two cannon by the 1st tee fire a thunderous salute. It is a ceremony of unparalleled power.

---

5 Tsar Peter it was who thus inaugurated Kümmel as the Golfer's Liqueur, having discovered it in 1696 at the Bols distillery in Holland where he acquired the recipe. This splendid tradition is carried on by the Mentzendorff company in the Loire Valley to this day.

THE AGM

The approach of the Annual General Meeting of a golf club is a time of unparalleled tension for the Captain, committee members and all appointed officers. An AGM can be a routine and relaxed affair, over in half an hour and followed by refreshments in the bar, or it can be a battlefield littered with casualties over whose bodies the conflict rages until terminated by a procedural guillotine or by sheer exhaustion. Sometimes the causes of conflict can be seen approaching: a proposed rise in subscriptions or the provision of a named parking place for the Lady Captain being notorious *casus belli*. Sometimes, however, the latent fury of members can blaze up over the most surprising issues such as the provision of heated ball washers or whether the ice in the Kummel should be blocked or crushed.

Royal St Lukes Golf Club, founded in 1603 and the world's oldest, is also the source of the country's earliest surviving golf club minutes. These are now conserved in the National Library in London and extracts from those of 1940, 1776 and especially the tempestuous AGM of 1650 are reproduced below by kind permission of the Trustees. Comparison of the seventeenth-century minutes with those of the twenty-first, shows how little has changed within the game. They show why the AGM is regarded by a certain species of member as unmissable, the best entertainment since the closure of the Colosseum in Rome, and for the same reasons.

The majority of men simply wish to pursue their lives in peace and tranquillity. However, there will always be those who are excited by the spectacle of gladiatorial armed combat – and by the terrifying sight of wild beasts roaming an arena in search of lunch. In times of peace, these men need an outlet for their bloodlust. These are the AGM men...

GOLF CLUBBE OF ST. LUKE IN THE COUNTY OF SUFFOLK

Know ye All and Sundry that; A Meetyng plenary of the said Clubbe within the Clubbehous was convened on the 14th day of July in the yeare of Grace 1650. Amen.

The Captane bade courteous welcome to the nine & eighty Members present.

Captane & Members stood uncovered for two minutes in pious Memory of the Members killed in the late Civil Warre - and in remembrance of Hys Majestie King Charles I, an Hon. Member of the Clubbe, lately beheaded before hys Palace of Whitehall.

The Royal Clubbes, being brought from hys Locker, were auctioned to Sir Toby Blackwoode in the sum of 28 L., the locker to be kept inviolate until G-d shall be pleased to grant Restoration of our monarchy.

The Treasurer & Remembrancer, being called, gave not a true account of the Accounts but would onlye say with great boldnesse that Expenditure had exceeded Income & straightway drew hys sword saying was there any Questions - whereupon Sir Thos. Wakeham rose & called hym a varlet & a villein & drew hys sword and closed with hym at which the Captane, crying order, Order! drew & fired his pistole in the aire which severed the corde causing the chandeliere to fall upon Col. Manningham, Jas. Haswell Esq., the Bishop of Derby, & others to their injury who, being incensed, the combatte became generall, & did erupt outwith the hous on to the 18th greene and there continued until the Captane, commanding the gate cannon to be discharged, brought order.

All being returned into the Hous, the Captane earnestlie desired the Members to refraine from violence, being mindful that many, being Royalist Cavaliers & Parliamentary Roundheddes, were but recently combatant in the long and hateful Civil Warre - & were unused to peece.

He then did call for questions to the Committee of the Greenes ,whereupon Marcus Fairchild Esq., rose & asked why a vaste lake of water yet remayned within the great bunker by the 12th greene to which Jas. Fairfax, Keeper of the Greene said, in insolence ,that as it came from G-d then He, that is, G-d, would remove it when He saw fitte whereupon Fairchild did say well then until such tyme can it be stokked with troute which, being fryed, Members might enjoy pending the usual endlesse wait for the 13th greene to clear, whereupon Sir Dudley Fortescue said that if neither G-d nor the greenekeepers will remove the water - then might it at leaste be changed?

Richard Pyke Esq., rose, saying that he & hys caddie together with all right-thinking golfyng men walked the course whyle playing. He said wherefore is Sir Percy Dowser Bt. suffered to swaye around in a Sedan Chaire carried by two liveried footmen & stuffed (Chaire & Baronet) with all manner of foode & drynk? - & furthermore by what right did Lord Marchmont, hys caddie, clubbemaker & mistresse lurch around the linkes within his carriage & four, followed by a pack of houndes - for the ruttes caused by Hys L'dship's carriage wheeles were as much a damned nuisance as the droppyngs of hys horses - & hys dogges for which he did move that Ld. Marchmont be charged therewith & roundly censured.

Whereupon Ld. Marchmont rose & called Pyke for a damned Roundhedde and turned hys back upon hym whereat Pyke did say, I be not affronted, Gentlemen, for verily I have seene hys back before! Aye, 'twas at the battle of Edgehill, wherefrom he did runne away! Whereat Ld. Marchmont did utter a great oathe & said he did not runne away but was onlye retreating, you kern, you gallowglass, How dare you speake thus to mee, a Peer of the Realme of ancient lineage & pedigree, you whose mother was but a Houndsditch washerwoman, you who cannot tracke your own ancestrie back to your father!

Whereat the Captane called Halte! & desired that they would all cease fyre & all would rise & drink a health to Oliver Cromwell, Lord Protector of England, at which Ld Marchmont with others swoare they would rather dye & flung their gauntlets before the Council & resygned saying they would embrace the Tennys.

There being no other Busyness, the Meetyng broke up in fair dysorder, the survyvyng Members being resolved to reconvene, unarmed, one yeare hence at two of the clock upon St. Swithin's Eve.

Attested, Signed & Sealed by me,

Edward Fellowes, Esq,
Hon. Secretar.

Down the centuries the St Luke's GC minutes chart the evolution of the Club and of the country, some of the entries recording historical events of seismic importance at home and abroad. For example in the Minutes of the AGM held on 18th Sept. 1776 we find: Motion;

That the Captain write forthwith to; Messrs. Benj. Franklin, Thos. Jefferson, Rev. John Witherspoon & other Overseas Members of the Club resident in Virginia, Massachusetts Bay and other British Colonies of N. America, warning that unless their Declaration of Independence is rescinded forthwith & they return to allegiance to the Crown, then not only will their Lockers be reallocated & the contents auctioned, but their rights to participation in the Spring and Autumn Meetings will be suspended sine die.

Moreover, being our good friends & colleagues, they should also be advised confidentially that they are liable to be suspended, not just by the Club – but also by the neck.

At the AGM held in the first desperate year of a later war and convened in the club's Anderson Shelter during a raid, a submitted written Motion shows that the national spirit shone on, undimmed.

August 14th 1940

Suggestion :

That, to permit play to resume, the heavy anti-aircraft batteries presently in the middle of the 2nd and 13th fairways be resited to the semi-rough and that the gunners be required to indicate by a whistle, bugle, or hoisted flag that they are about to open fire.

Furthermore, that unexploded bombs, parachute mines etc., be surrounded by a white circle of radius 50 yds. & clearly marked 'GUR – UXB' – so that detonation will not inconvenience play.

Penalty for taking cover during bombing, strafing and other disgraceful enemy activities – 2 strokes.

Sgd. Brig. G.V. Barrington, DSO

Response: **Agreed.**

THE LADIES – AND THEIR CAPTAIN

Your Lady Captain is, and has to be, a woman of sterling worth and warm yet seismic personality. Not only must she keep her own battalion in order, she must also deal with the men's perennial suspicions and locker-room mutterings that a tee-time takeover and a clubhouse makeover is imminent. She will chair the Ladies Committee, attended by the men's Captain and the Secretary, at which all sources of real and potential conflict and combat will be settled, usually to her satisfaction. She will be a feminist in the sense that a degree of active, occasionally militant, feminism is required in the early stages to redress ancient discriminations. However, when the men have come to their senses over the disposition of the clubhouse facilities and the general *modus operandi* of the club, she will be seen to be a fair and loyal democrat. She will apply the common-sense solution of a private room for breast-feeding amid the uproar when it was Suggested[1] for the mixed Lounge and will have applauded the splendid letter to *The Times* supporting the Admiralty's bombardment of the BBC for persistently describing ships not as 'she' but as 'it'.

She will have watched the admission of women to most golf clubs and listened with wry amusement to the Captain of a famous London club admitting that indeed they had no lady members, but that was simply because none had *applied*. If one did, the Captain had continued, marching steadily into the quicksand, her application would necessarily fail; not because she was a *woman*, you understand, but because she was *not* a man!

When the AGM discusses the appointment of a first lady President for the club, the Lady Captain will observe that the United Kingdom has a female Head of State and has had a female Prime Minister. She will recall that resistance to the first election of a woman to the House of Commons[2] had dissolved in laughter, always the most potent means of clearing a logjam. This was when an M.P. rose to say:

'Mr. Speaker, I personally would welcome the presence of a young woman in this House, since it will help to balance the number of old women here already!'

Your Lady Captain is likely to be a firm supporter of the Ladies Golf Union (LGU) the governing body for women's and girls' amateur golf in the UK and the Republic of Ireland. As in certain other sports such as hockey and rugby, Ireland in this context means the whole island, the border between the Irish Republic and Northern Ireland being declared invisible. The Union thus represents some 200,000 lady golfers in the geographical British Isles, dealing with everything from all-Britain and Ireland tournaments to the local promotion of the game to girls. It is thus admirable.

---

1   i.e. placed in the Suggestion Book.
2   Nancy Witcher Astor, Viscountess Astor CH (1879 – 1964) She entered the House in 1919 as Conservative MP for Plymouth.

Headquartered at St.Andrews, it was founded in 1893 by Miss Issette Pearson, the remarkable and indomitable woman who became its first Secretary. It runs the annual Home International Matches involving the four home nations and the great Curtis Cup matches against the USA. This is the ladies counterpart of the Walker Cup and is held in the June of 'even' years, some three months before each Ryder Cup.

The first British Ladies Championship was held at the (not-yet Royal) Lytham & St Annes Golf Club in that same year of 1893 and was won by Lady Margaret Scott, daughter of the Earl of Eldon who beat Issette Pearson 7 and 5 in the Final. The Championship was a great success, despite the curmudgeonly and dire predictions of old Horace Hutchison, writing in *Golf*, a weekly newspaper; '*Women are constitutionally & physically unfitted for golf... never have & never can unite to push any scheme to success... bound to fall out... bound to quarrel at the slightest provocation. This first Ladies' Championship*' boomed Horace, '*will be the last!*'

And so it was – until the next year at Littlestone in Kent and the next at Royal Portrush in Co. Antrim and so on through 1947 when Mildred 'Babe' Didrikson Zaharias became the first American to win it – and on to the Centenary in 1993, held fittingly at its original home, the now Royal Lytham & St Annes.

Two years after Lady Scott triumphed at Lytham, Lucy Barnes Brown of the famous Shinnecock Hills Golf Club on Long Island won the inaugural US Ladies Amateur Championship. This was an 18-hole strokeplay event in which thirteen competitors played, or rather groped their way around a fog-bound Meadow Brook GC at Hempstead, NY. The following year at the Morris County Club in New Jersey, the format was switched to match play and a Scottish element entered, or rather ended, the competition which was won by Beatrix Hoyt, also of Shinnecock Hills.

Robert Cox was a golf course designer and MP for Edinburgh South who had learned the game on the ancient links of Musselburgh while boarding at Loretto School in the town. Cox donated to the USGA the Cup which bears his name and is to this day, awarded to the winner of the US Ladies Amateur Championship. The Cup is actually a magnificent Etruscan vase decorated with scenes of St Andrews, of whose university Cox was a graduate. He was rewarded by the USGA with a silver cleek; 'for his efforts in promoting the ancient game in the United States'. The most successful lady amateur in the Championship's history was Glenna Collett Vare who won six times between 1922 and 1935 and was described by Gene Sarazen as 'the greatest woman golfer of all time'. That has to be balanced, however, by England's Joyce Wethered who won the Ladies Amateur Championship four times, the English Amateur five times in a row and was described by Bobby Jones, no less, as 'the finest golfer I have ever seen'.

At Cromer in Norfolk in 1905, two very special American ladies had competed in the Ladies Amateur Championship Harriet and Margaret Curtis were both former US amateur champions who played out of the Essex County Club in Manchester, Mass. It was customary at that time for the Home International matches to precede the Championship, only this time there was a difference. The four countries having had their competition, a combined team was put up to take on the visiting Americans in an informal match. Here the Curtis sisters conceived the idea, which came to birth in 1932, of the great biennial match for the cup which bears their name.

But to return to the Lady Captain and her charges. She will have agreed with the Admiral who was challenged by a lady BBC interviewer as to *why* ships should be the only inanimate objects to have a gendered pronoun and be accounted female and not neuter. The old seadog thundered:

'When HM the Queen Mother launched HMS *Ark Royal*, she did not say 'may God bless *it* – and all who sail in *it*!' Women and ships, Madam, share one central, key characteristic.'

'And just what might that be, Admiral?'

'They are both *wonderful*. Good day.'

Indeed they are. Women are an ornament to the greatest game. They invest the links with colour and the clubhouse with gaiety and decorum. They demonstrate that a driver does not have to be swung at warp speed to achieve distance. They bring order to the AGM and common sense to the trumpeting in the Suggestion Book. In many ways they are tougher than men, living on average of seven years longer than their male partners – mainly due to their general avoidance of excessive carnivorous eating, drinking of coloured fluids and inhalation of rolled-up plants.

And above all, there is their great feat. In just 270 days a woman can produce from a single cell, ten times smaller than a pinhead, the most complex object in the known universe. This object comprises 20 trillion cells organised into 16 integrated organ systems and is surmounted by a supercomputer with a 600 Gb memory. When it is further considered that she does this almost always without error and moreover delivers it on time and *alive*, then beside this colossal achievement the male contribution to the process is seen for what it is – a pale and ephemeral thing.

Your Lady Captain and her troops do not labour, metaphorically, the above points. They simply reflect quietly that they can proudly trace their golfing ancestry to a great Queen and First Lady of golf. Through her the women's game began by Royal Command, in contrast to the men's game which was probably originated by an hairy Pict whacking a pebble into a rabbit hole with a discarded deer antler.

'What would men be without women?' the great Twain was asked.

'Scarce, Sir, *mighty* scarce' was the sage's sage reply.

THE OLDEST MEMBER

At 89, Harry Carruthers has been the Oldest Member of the club (OM) for several months since the burial of his great friend Col. George Trubshaw who, having just entered his 90th year, was sadly required to leave it again after losing a final bout with tertiary malaria. The Colonel's funeral had been conducted by the Rev. Augustus James, club chaplain, who had convulsed the post-interment wake by recounting the pre-funeral briefing he had received from the martial corpse. Trubshaw had specified the hymns, the prayers, the incidental (military) music, the firing party, the piper's lament and was moving on to the precise content of the eulogy when the exasperated Rev. finally said, 'Look Trubby, why don't *I* get into the coffin and *you* conduct the show!'

The Colonel had been lowered into mother earth clutching 'The Grand Piano' his massive, ancient and trusty driver, surrounded by a full set of hickory-shafted woods and irons. Although officially C of E and hopefully destined for Paradise, the old campaigner who was always a believer in Plan B, went down with a £2 coin in his mouth to pay Charon the ferryman for his journey across the Styx. 'For remember, Harry,' he had said softly to Carruthers near the end, 'no plan survives contact with the Enemy!'

So the mantle of OM fell across the broad, straight shoulders of Henry G. Carruthers, late of Her Majesty's Diplomatic Service and now curmudgeon-in-chief of the club. As OM he is expected to act as the sounding board against which all new fangled innovations are thrown, and as often thrown back. The OM is a member *ex-officio* of the Executive & General Purposes Committee and is the guardian of tradition, standards and general rectitude on and off the course. His window seat in Members Lounge gives him both a geographical and a moral view across the course and around the clubhouse. The Suggestion Book lies on its table close to his right hand, and woe betide the member who seeks to inscribe a comment or complaint without the OM's knowledge and assent.

Dress in clubhouse and on the course is naturally a major issue for him. He gave way, eventually, over the popular 'dirty bar' but it's still collar & tie for lunch in the dining room, and used to be for breakfast as well. A visitor, staying in the Dormy House, had once abreacted sharply on being told of the then strict dress code. 'Look here, chief steward' said he with some heat, '*surely* a gentleman can eat breakfast wearing a sports shirt, but with a tailored jacket on top and trousers. *Surely!*' And the chief steward had said, 'Certainly, Sir. A gentleman would indeed be able to eat breakfast wearing a sports shirt, tailored jacket and trousers – but not *here*.'

Dress on the golfcourse is another OM speciality. The Starter is strictly charged not to let players drive off the 1st tee wearing (a) reversed or sideways-pointing baseball caps (b) round-necked T-shirts (c) *any* shirt in the colours of a Premier Division soccer team and, most importantly (d) shorts unaccompanied by long hose[1] to the kneecap. In the last case, the OM's binoculars are kept handy to adjudicate. The player in question is made to stand facing the clubhouse and then to slowly pirouette twice, raising one leg at a time. With the Starter's telescope trained on the clubhouse windows, the verdict is conveyed by the OM's raising of a green or red handkerchief. It is, naturally, final.

The only exception to the football shirt rule had been made in the case of the late and much missed US Open champion Payne Stewart., inaugurating the second course with demonstration matches with the home professional. Stewart was then under contract to advertise the National Football League of the United States by wearing the colours of one of its constituent teams. It had been patiently explained by the Secretary to the then OM that this was OK. American football was an evolved variant of rugby and Stewart's colourful green and white ensemble represented a team.

'So, who is he today?' demanded the OM, gazing out at the brilliant spectacle.

'I am given to understand,' said the Secretary, consulting the events programme, 'that this morning he is a dolphin of Miami.'

'A dolphin of Miami' mused the OM, 'How *extraordinary*. Tell me, Mr Secretary, will he change into another team, or indeed mutate into another creature, for the afternoon round?'

'He will indeed. I believe that after lunch he will become a ram of Los Angeles...'

The Oldest Member recalls his earliest days as a junior member in the 1930s when gentlemen played in Oxford bags, addressed each other by surname and carried clubs which were un-numbered but named: driver and brassie, spoon and mashie, jigger and baffy. He remembers that they smoked pipes and wore ties on the course and Henry Cotton came here in his Bentley and you could fill up your own Hillman or Morris for ten shillings and the sun never set on the Empire, whereas *now...* but at this point the sleep of the just, and the just alive, will overtake him as the noble head droops and the *Telegraph* slowly slips to the floor.

---

1   Hose. From Anglo-Saxon *hosa* – a stocking.

At least, the OM will opine on awakening, at least the R&A still rules the golfing world, except for the Colonists and the Mexicans, but as for the rest, well, life is becoming progressively incomprehensible. He can understand the new 'green' logic behind the new solar-powered vacuum thunderboxes in the Gents from which solid waste is piped to the Artisans Club down the road, but cannot conceive what they would do with it. Equally, he is bemused by the mandatory re-routing of the seaside 12th fairway to accommodate the breeding ground of the threatened elephant hawk moth (*Deilephila elpenor*) of whose existence, let alone endangerment, he had been unaware. The recent *dictat* from the Healthy & Safe Executive that caddies must now wear armoured vests and steel helmet has left him in a state of alarm, particularly as the latter resemble the old *Wehrmacht* coalscuttle variety at which, as recently as seventy years ago, the OM had been in the habit of opening fire.

The club's annual dinner is his *forte*. He is always invited by the Captain to give the Loyal Toast, being quietly reminded on the night: 'Now remember, OM, it's *not* 'The King...' At weekends, and at the Secretary's gentle insistence, two of the youngest members are always placed to flank the OM at lunch with instructions to bring the old boy out on the pre-war club and on his last Hewitt at Deal and those warm bygone summers with the broom in bloom and the sweet waft of scythed grass and the echoes of epic matches between strong men long gone to their rest.

Such was Freddy Cartwright who is the subject of his favourite, much told story: how Freddy had never once been on the green in regulation at the Road Hole at St Andrews, but *always* in the terrifying road bunker; how his will specified that his ashes would be scattered, at night, upon that green; how his sons loyally did his bidding, but just as the urn was opened and upended, how a gust of wind came from the north and, stone me, but was he not back in the bunker *again*!

Judge not the OM too harshly. One day...

THE CLUB BORE

Αnd then, would you believe, at the 13th…,' and you're all in for another torture session as he drives off, again into the left rough, embarking on yet another hole of a long ago round with the late Bertie Cadwallader and 'that chap, who was it now? I can see him… Well anyway, I was left with 200 yards to the flag so I said to Williams my caddy I said, Williams, wake up. *Williams!* I've got 200 to go…'

We've all heard it. We've all suffered from it. Naturally, none of us has been guilty of it, being able to hear ourselves as others hear us. However it, and he, is part of the clubhouse furniture, part of the past, part of the present. Indeed dealing with the bore is an essential part of the training in good manners through which we all have to go. Out on the course, the bore is effectively neutralised since we only congregate on tees and greens, when there are more important matters in hand. But in the clubhouse, watch out.

They come in all shapes and sizes and wait, crouched or coiled like carnivorous predators, to pounce upon the unwary. You will meet them on trains, boats and planes, sometimes at funerals, often at weddings, always at drinks parties and, heaven forfend, even when trapped in supermarket checkout queues. That is not to say they will not appear out of the blue, or rather the mist, on a mountain-top or from a woodland glade, for they have the power of materialising anywhere.

The best-dressed examples are to be found in the smart gentlemen's clubs of Mayfair and St James's, with heaven knows how many more in the several thousand golf clubs scattered throughout the land. Every club can boast its unique example. They seem to be an unavoidable ingredient of the members' lounge, that inner sanctum to which they belong, their numbers acting as a litmus test of the vitality of the club's membership.

Now, it would be a fine thing if at first glance we could recognise the characteristics of the bore, but sadly that just isn't nature's way: red in tooth and jaw, it somehow demands that we suffer. Although they appear in all guises – young, old, male and female – the most common variant of all is, predictably, the male of those intransient and intransigent middle years. This is a species so well set in its ways, habits and speech patterns that were it raining steaming pumice outside, or were extraterrestrials to land on the practice green on a *non*-visitors day, they would hardly take notice.

One prevailing characteristic true bores share is that they invariably see and represent themselves as informed and eloquent upon their subject. Adopting a quasi-scholarly mode of speech and gesture, they are happy to discuss in terrifying detail the thorny question of golf's rules and regulations, plus any arcane aspect of its history and evolution. They will discourse upon whence it came, how it developed and, worst of all, where in heaven's name, they ask you, is it *going*? The more recondite the issue the greater the certainty, the more profound the question the more facile the answer; and the more facile the answer the greater the time devoted to its exposition. A little knowledge and a self-inflated sense of authority are a lethal combination.

The problem is that the true bore sees himself as 'the enlightened one' and his subject as one of universal fascination. He knows that he is the *fons et origo* of illumination upon it, whereas non-golfers and the club wits see him as not only numbingly time-consuming but diabolically tedious. Obviously it is difficult to cope with these tormented souls who are the only members of the club who can cause happiness simply by leaving the room. Whilst leaving the room at speed oneself may appear rude, it may be the only course of action which will preserve one's temper and indeed good manners. Most bores, however, are too thick-skinned to take notice of such evasive action since once on a roll, and provided the audience doesn't fall below one, there is little on God's earth that can stop them.

Worse still, it's impossible to spot them until it is too late. The stranger you find sitting opposite you in the club lounge may suddenly change. He who only a moment ago appeared to be a congenial companion will inexplicably move mid-stream from a dialogue on a shared topic of mutual interest to a suspiciously fluent monologue. The subject may be the grip, the long-handled putter, even the 'Spitfire' that unlamented ball of the 60s which had the unnerving propensity to divide in two when struck[1].

But most ominously of all, he will suddenly inhale, pout like a Gobi fish and mention the word 'grasses'. It is then, if you've any sense left, that you realise your hellish predicament and look nervously round for a door, an open window, anything through which to tumble free and make for sanctuary. It's remarkable how the appearance of the word 'Fescue' triggers this response, especially if couched in the phrase 'Take fescue, now...' It is just a blade of grass, but able to clear a room. For the agronomical bore is the deadliest of all. When the fescue pokes through the surface and bores its way into the conversation, then for everyone else it's just too late. He continues, 'You've really got to get down on your hands and knees to appreciate the stuff, you've got to feel it and touch it'. He rolls his eyes and pauses airily. 'Fescue, of course, is natural to links golf, but mix it with a bit of Red Bent, particularly on a green, then you've really

---

1   The Rules Committee suggested that in such cases play should continue with 'the larger half'.

got something special: fast, firm and rapidly regenerative'. He ploughs on, heedless of the furrows being raised on watching brows. 'Then again, there's the Bermuda variety, a heavily bladed grass grown mostly in the Americas and warmer climes, perfect for target golf, perfect for the lobwedge, but then again look at the advent of meadow grass on our fairways...'

He eats, sleeps and talks golf and its grasses like the snooker aficionado discussing the offside rule or the rod & line man who *knows* the best type of nymph to cast on still water when the mayflies swarm – and who believes that Moby Dick is essentially a treatise on angling.

The problem of grasses, which this book has deliberately ignored, goes back such a long way that there are innumerable agronomical issues to rovide fuel for a soliloquy. Thus our bore is absolutely in his element in the comfort of the clubroom, large gin in hand, while the rest of us simply want to get out there and smash it.

'Remember,' he pouts, 'the grass will always point towards the sun. So, if you're putting against the sun, you really must stroke the ball a little firmer than usual and, as Willie Park said, 'a man that can putt is a match for anyone'.

'Now, which of the many Willie Parkses was that?' one of the victims will hazard, desperate to stem or at least slow the flow. Not for long. He will say decisively, 'It was the Willie Park who said, 'A man who can putt...''

The one thing that the club bore cannot abide is being sat with the Club's wags and wits. The trouble is that they don't want to sit with the bore, although the combination can occasionally be vastly entertaining. And talking of wits, none handled bores more deftly than the late Oscar Wilde who was accosted by one at a London party with, 'Ah, it's Mr Wilde. I passed your house the other day.'

'Thank you very much *indeed*.'

THE BANDIT

The Bandit is a member of your golf club, because every golf club has at least one, and every one has a golf club. He may not be masked and carry a stiletto, but can still usually be identified, sometimes in the clubhouse and certainly at the annual prize-giving. His handicap is a mystery, always curiously higher than his level of play seems to justify, but then again his strokeplay returns never quite justify a reduction. Of course they don't. Because his game is matchplay – and you are the target.

Bandit spotting is a fine art which takes years to learn but is always worth the effort. Like all good confidence men the bandit will initially seem normal and indeed charming. He may well have a wife, children and a steady job, his family and colleagues entirely unaware of the secret life he leads at the club. He gives no outward sign of banditry: there are no hand-tooled alligator golf shoes, no flash of a diamond tooth and certainly no visible dorsal fin. Should you encounter him within your own club, or at an inter-club match, you'll be the target of a standard bout of amateur golf banditry as described below. However, watch out when on holiday in Iberia or Las Vegas or any international watering hole, because there you may encounter the real McCoy, a professional from the premier division of tiger sharks who roam the golfing seas.

Such a man was the legendary John Montague who once beat Bing Crosby in a one-hole match using only a baseball bat, a shovel and a rake. This was at Lakeside Golf Club, close by the film studios of Burbank. There was a substantial bet riding on the match in which Crosby, a fine golfer, would play the par-4 hole with his regular clubs while Montague would drive with the bat, play his approach with the shovel and putt using the rake handle as a billiard cue. Crosby parred the hole – and lost.

Alvin 'Titanic' Thompson was another unsinkable gentleman hustler who might have done well on the 1930s pro tour in America, but couldn't afford even to make the cut, since he could not afford the cut in income. Thompson would win a big money game, then seem to take pity on his opponent and offer to play him again for double the stake, this time left-handed. The opponent, unaware that Thompson was naturally a southpaw would leap at the chance, only to crash again. A good friend of the BBC's Alastair Cooke of *Letter from America* fame, Ti Thompson was ever the sporting winner. He never crushed his adversaries. If they shot 90 he'd shoot 89 – but if they shot 70, he'd be 69.

He was what is known as a proposition gambler. In other words he would propose a seemingly impossible task and offer temptingly long odds against managing it, having secretly swung those odds right round, past evens, and into his favour. For example, having had a wintertime bet well taken up that he could drive a golf ball 500 yards, he embarked his victims in a fleet of cars and drove them from the clubhouse to a tee. He then addressed the ball, suddenly switching his aim from the fairway to a nearby frozen lake, across which a single Titanic drive secured the cash.

Back at club level, signs of banditry can be detected as early as the first tee. The sight of a 1-iron in your opponent's bag should set off an initial alarm, given Lee Trevino's famous crack that it's the safest thing to hold aloft in a thunderstorm, since not even God can hit a 1-iron. You may also notice that his bag is unusually slim. Bandits like pencil bags, usually with several good luck charms dangling from them. There will also be a couple of visitor tags from championship courses such as Turnberry and Birkdale which he'll have murdered but won't mention, initially. He'll have a complex system of marking his balls, using a monogrammed felt-tipped pen. Even his ball-marker will likely display a coat of arms unlikely to be his own.

His proposal of what seems to be an overly complex betting arrangement on the game is another warning sign. He'll start with the basic Nassau; so much on the outward nine, same on the inward, double on the final result. So far so good – but the true bandit will rapidly escalate the stakes with a blizzard of oozlers, fizzlers, sandies, porkos, camels and birdies – plus presses and multipliers, till a CA firm would be hard put to account for it all. Remember, the more he piles on, the more confident he is of taking you.

So there you are, already in his sights and playing his game and you're still no farther than the 1st tee. But it is right there on the tee that it really begins, and it is on the 18th tee, if the game's still alive, that it will end. On the greens, the experienced bandit will never do anything so crude as to tap his white golf shoes while you're putting. On the fairways, he will not draw your attention to the 'roughest rough on the course over there' and he would never stoop to coughing, coin jangling or permitting the emission of any audible gaseous eructation from any orifice – especially that one – while you address an approach. No, the damage will be done on the tee, for the tee is the cockpit of banditry.

Golf is not a contact sport. The bandit can't rugby-tackle you, or sledge[1] you as in cricket. He can't menace you with any part of his equipment or fire a shot at you. It's an own-ball game, so he can't hit, touch or even mark yours. Golf is a mind game, a form of open-air chess. He has to get at your mindset through language, and that means both body language and English. Crude and cheap shots such as '*never* seen you play so *well*' or 'never seen you play so *badly*' are just too well known to be used now, and are in fact more a form of cheating than banditry. No, it'll be more subtle and sophisticated.

---

1 Sledging; The art of discomfiting batsmen by pointed references to their parentage, physical & mental deficiencies, wifely infidelities and general incompetence. Brought to a pitch of perfection, such as that at Lord's, by The Convicts when playing The Mother Country.

'High time they moved those OB posts back a bit' is a regular bandit gambit on the tee, before which you may not have even registered the white death-markers, now frighteningly close. Another ploy on the tee of a longish par-4 is for him to pull out an iron. He then leans casually on it while you, who have the honour, look with mounting uncertainty at the driver in your hands. These seeds of doubt germinate fast and when your drive has exhibited a boomerang hook, the iron will disappear and a dead straight siege-gun drive will flash away.

On a shortish par-4 the tactic is different. While you prepare to drive you'll hear him say to his 'caddy' or partner, who is in fact a primed accomplice, 'Think we can get it on again, today?' to which the partner in crime will say, 'Sure. Nice easy swing and bring it in from the left, just like last week.' This propels you to a massive effort with driver resulting in a sliced banana, whereupon he pops a 3-wood straight down to within wedge-range of the green.

Incidentally, watch out for unsolicited confidential comments from his caddy which will be aimed at further seed sowing, e.g., 'He hasn't played much since Open Final Qualifying…' or, for a rather older bandit, 'Not bad, eh, for a man with a quadruple bypass and one lung…' and so on.

The correct treatment of a bandit is never to play with him again and to tell the story to your friends. But that doesn't help you out on the course where the best plan as always is to ignore him, take it back slow and rhythmic, pause at the top, follow through – and stuff him at least 3 and 2. Then give him a real bonecrushing orthopaedic handshake on the 16th green, smile broadly and tell him, 'Thank you *so* much. What a *pleasure* that[2] was.'

2 i.e. The handshake (unspoken)

Advice to U.S. Citizens visiting the British Isles for Golf & related Purposes

American visitors are most welcome on British and especially Scottish golf courses. This is largely because the Scots unshakeably believe that their emigrants to the thirteen North American colonies were responsible for the U.S. Constitution, the War of Independence and the Declaration thereof. Actually, the latter is only half true since only twenty-three of the fifty-six Signers on 4 July 1776 were Scots or of Scots ancestry. They were, however, certainly responsible for the export of the game to North America as described above.

While preparing to leave the US it's a good idea to get a flavor (remembering to add a 'u' when over here) of what awaits by reading Shakespeare's *Henry V* or *The Wind in the Willows* by Kenneth Grahame, while a look at *Monty Python and the Knights who say 'Ni!'* will give a real feel for our early history.

On arrival in England, prepare at once to make the switch from driving on the right (wrong) side of the road to the left (right) side. If this is too radical, just drive down the median with the Stars & Stripes streaming proudly through the sunroof. With the roof open, one of the first things you'll notice is the cool temperature and the lovely low humidity. In parts of the States life is uncomfortable in Summer without an air-conditioned home, office and car, whereas the UK is an air-conditioned *country*. This partly explains the relative lack of showers, the vast majority of which descend from rain clouds which, fear not, are in plentiful supply. After his first round on the Old Course, that fine US golfer Ed Furgol, winner of the 1954 US Open, came up from the locker room to the atrium of the R&A clubhouse at St Andrews, wearing only a towel and a puzzled expression.

'Sir,' he said to the Chief Steward, 'I cannot find the showers and I've looked everywhere. OK, so where are they at?'

'Showers? There's no shower here, Sir'.

'Really. No *showers*? So what do you guys, like, *do*?'

'A member of this Club, Sir, would gae hame tae his castle, should he perceive, or be advised o' a need tae *bathe...*'

You may also notice, it's hard not to, that in summer British seaside links courses go brown. Do not be alarmed. This is not a failure of greenkeeping, it's Nature. The greens and tees will be kept green by watering, but many of us believe the fairways should be allowed to brown up as they've done for thousands of years. The grass may look moribund but it's very much alive. The colour change is simply due to the loss of green chlorophyll pigment, as the plant sends its roots down a further six inches to get at the moisture. You'll recall that in 2006 as he cradled the Claret Jug, your very own Mr Woods made a particular point of congratulating the greenkeeping staff of the *very* brown Royal Liverpool course at Hoylake. Indeed, many of us feel that fairway watering of our links courses should be left to the Almighty – the original, and best, head greenkeeper.

Some American guests find the food and drink tricky. You all know what to do with smoked salmon and Aberdeen Angus steaks and you certainly enjoy Scotch on the rocks, but what about the porridge on the clubhouse breakfast menu at Carnoustie? Try it at least once and take it with a pinch of salt. Porridge is made from oatmeal which you like over there. It puts hair on your chest, fire in your belly and iron in your soul. It may look like moistened plasterboard and taste like it too, but porridge fuelled the men who crossed oceans to open up Canada and Australia and who, six centuries ago, brought to birth the great field game which unites us all. It is thus a dish of pure character. Close your eyes, and enjoy.

Pronunciation is important. The UK's capital city is London, not *Londonengland*. We know it needs to be distinguished from London, North Dakota, but London itself is capable of doing just that, as are *Parisfrance, Romitaly* and your other favourite European watering holes. In Scotland, the capital city is pronounced 'Edinburra.' Do not call it 'Edinburg' unless you come from Pittsburra. If, on the other hand, you're a Texas rancher do be cautious when describing the size of your property, since in the Scottish Highlands the average size of a farm, or *croft*, is about four acres.

'I can be in the car all mornin' and still not reach the other side of my spread,' a visiting Amarillo rancher declared to a golfing crofter, who nodded sympathetically and said,

'Sorry am I to hear that! But man, I know just how you feel – did I not have a car like that myself once.'

If at all possible, hire a caddy. He will carry your bag but he does not carry subtitles, and the Scots dialect is powerful. So when he says, 'Ach, ye've gien yerrsel a gey besom o' a pitch fae therr,'[1] just nod wisely and extend your hand, palm up. The correct implement will be inserted into it. Never, ever, argue with a Scots caddy over club selection. The raising of just one eyebrow by a fraction of an inch will be taken as a mortal insult, and may have consequences.

---

1   Sadly, you have left yourself a rather difficult pitch from that position.

Most important of all: remember that if in Scotland you are not, repeat not, in England. The Scots had a War of Independence with England too, culminating in 1314 with a home win in a massive two-day strokeplay event at a place called Bannockburn. Mention this daily and your stock among the locals will soar. Relations with England have been generally friendly for over 400 years now, since Queen Elizabeth I nominated Scotland's monarch as her successor. And so it was that in 1603 King James VI betook himself, his court and Mr Mayne, his 'clubbe & balle maker' to London. Four years later, having identified his most argumentative subjects, he packed them off to Jamestown, Virginia, little knowing what he was starting – but that's another story.

Above all, as a US visitor, do avoid the natural instinct to let your jaw drop and your eyes glaze over when you: (a) discover that petrol (gas) is sold in litres at the equivalent of $6.50 a gallon; (b) order a beer expecting a cold lager and get a pint of warm brown fluid with things floating in it; or (c) hear that the BBC are thinking seriously about a 24-hour cricket channel.

We are pleased to be able to direct the above helpful remarks to potential visitors from the States with which most of us have some personal connections, Mr Dodd for example having a delightful Californian wife. My own first contact was a Summer's attachment as a student at the Medical School of the University of Michigan at Ann Arbor. I also have the pleasure of belonging to the Dinner Match Society, an assemblage of New England golfers dedicated to the finer points of golf, dining and not least to the reintroduction of the grand old foursomes game to their homeland [2].

I am also pleased to have been born at all. This is because in 1944, some years before I arrived, my father was lining up a long approach to a par-5 on an Ayrshire golf course when he was near-missed by a Boeing B-17 Flying Fortress being ferried in from the States. Subjected to headwinds on the long transatlantic crossing and out of fuel just short of Prestwick airfield, the American ferry pilot brought off an expert wheels-up landing which ended with a huge ground-loop just short of the green. There was no fire, there being not a drop of fuel left in the bomber's tanks. The American crew were climbing out, shaken but unhurt, only to be confronted by Dad who rapped sharply on the fuselage with his cleek enquiring equally sharply, 'Did you not see that I was about to play?'

'Sorry, Sir,' said the pilot, grinning ruefully as he surveyed the damage to plane and fairway. 'Well, anyway,' said my old man, 'welcome to Scotland.'

And welcome to you too.

---

2   Strictly the 2-ball alternate shot game, as played in the Ryder Cup.

GOLF GOES SOUTH: ENGLAND (AND SUNNINGDALE)

I t has been long believed that the 'long' game of golf on links or heathland as we presently know it, arrived in England with King James in 1603 and indeed it probably did. There was, however another game to which golf historians refer as the 'short game' which may well have been there for centuries. The famous Crécy window in the east transept of Gloucester Cathedral showing a man swinging at a small stationary ball[1], has been securely dated to the late 14th century. It possibly depicts that shorter game which may well be related to the *choule* of Flanders or *Jeu de Crosse* in northern France which has been thoroughly researched, at last, by the Dutch sports historians Geert & Sara Nijs[2]. However, what distinguishes all these games from modern golf is that they were played towards a vertical target, be it a temporary post in the ground, a tree, or a church door. The Scots, long used to turning things over in the hope of a better outcome, turned over the target from vertical to horizontal and, ever cautious about money, came up with the much cheaper and hence deeply satisfying concept of a target which was not present, but essentially absent – in other words, a hole.

In the correspondence of Catherine of Aragon, wife No. I of Henry VIII, there is a fascinating reference to golf being played by the king's subjects. Here is the queen writing to Thomas Wolsey the royal almoner and later Cardinal, who was away campaigning with Henry in France – and in the process of trashing Thérouanne in the Pas de Calais:

Master Almoner, from hence I have nothing to write to you that you be not so busy in this war as we be encumbered with it. I mean that touching my own concerns, for going further, when I shall not so often hear from the King. And all his subjects be very glad, I thank God, to be busy with the golf, for they take it as a pastime; my heart is very good to it, and I am horribly busy making standards, banners and bagets.

Often described as retiring and ineffectual, Queen Catherine was anything but. Regent of England in Henry's absence, she was tireless in superintending the fitting out of the army with which Thomas Howard, Earl of Surrey, advanced to Flodden Edge on the Border. There Surrey soundly defeated the Scots, killing James IV whose bloody surcoat Catherine proudly mailed to her husband in France. King James had paid the price for the playing of golf in his homeland. For it was English and Welsh arrows which, unopposed by Scots bowmen, did much of the execution at Flodden, the Scots having cheerfully ignored edict after edict appealing to them to give up weekend golf and practice their archery.

---

1   The player's stance is closed and his grip too strong – clearly a hooker.
2   G & S Nijs; *The Non-Royal but most Ancient Game of Crosse* (2008). Editions Geert and Sarah Nijs.

A century later a Scottish king again arrived at Flodden from Edinburgh, but this time did not halt. Bound for London and the Union of the Crowns was the man described by Sir Anthony Weldon as 'the wisest Fool in Christendom'. An enthusiastic golfer of unknown handicap, James VI & I caused his Palace of Eltham to become in effect the first Royal clubhouse as the game took root and flourished on the nearby Blacke Heathe, its inaugural home in England. In 2008 in the Painted Hall at Greenwich, a gala dinner of the Royal Blackheath Golf Club celebrated the quatercentenary of the game on the heath and in the Home Counties, the toast to 'The Blackheath Goffer' being proposed by David Harrison, Captain of the R&A.

Slowly but surely and with growing enthusiasm, England took up the game. Here new terrains for golf had to be established since linksland is relatively scarce south of the Border. Heathland, parkland and meadowland were recruited to supply territory, thus adding a certain new and dangerous phenomenon to the golfing picture. This was the tree – an object virtually unknown on the linksland – whose trunk, branches and foliage were to provide yet another major obstruction to the flight of errant drives. To this day the woods bordering English parkland courses echo to the clonk of direct hits and to the sound of whacked recoveries and ritual imprecations.

And so, English men and women discovered a field game that, unlike cricket, could be played in all seasons of the year, in most weathers and by persons of all ages from nine to ninety. It also appealed to the English instinct for fair play through the handicapping system. In many sports it is simply not possible for players of greatly differing standards to play against each other; imagine a tennis match with every game starting at 30-love in favour of the poorer player. Golf allows the equalisation of talent. While the better player may win more often, this is by no means certain, with the strokes being awarded precisely at those more difficult holes where the better player is at greater advantage.

By the beginning of the twentieth century golf was all over England and the 'Great Triumvirate' of Braid, Vardon and Taylor who dominated the Opens of that era featured appropriately and respectively: a Scotsman, a Jerseyman and an Englishman. Innovations started to flow from south to north. The oldest Collegiate golfing society on earth is the Oxford & Cambridge, founded in 1898 and which was followed by the Scottish Universities Golfing Society eight years later. The two societies do battle on an irregular basis but with just the same passion as did their ancestors at Bannockburn and Flodden. At a recent contest held at Sunningdale the teams arrived to find, open in the glass case in the hall, the Club's day-book for the year 1910. It had been carefully opened at a particular page wherein lay the results of the inaugural match between the Societies nigh on a hundred years before. It was in the handwriting of Harry S. Colt, Sunningdale's then Secretary and one of the finest golf course designers England has ever produced.[3]

---

3   The result was a 6-6 tie but was recorded as a win for OCGS! Colt, a Cambridge man, had succumbed to the good golfer's difficulty in counting beyond 5.

Collaboration across the Border was now the order of the day. Scots professionals found good work at course designers, keepers of the green and professionals in England, a classic example being Sunningdale itself. Here on the Surrey-Berkshire border and on a stretch of mixed heathland bordered by gorse, heather and pine, the Roberts brothers had spotted the potential for a great golf course. And so it came to pass that in the year 1900, forty years after Willie Park Sr. of Musselburgh won the first Open Championship, down to Sunningdale came his son, imaginatively named Willie Park Jr. of Musselburgh[4]. His hauntingly beautiful Old course, though extensively revised, is there to this day and was joined in 1923 by Harry Colt's New Course which is felt by many to be an even tougher test than the Old.

England also introduced new ideas on competitions, one of which is our harbinger of Spring and the new golf season. While our American cousins have a saying 'Another Spring, another Masters' and lead off the season with four rounds of strokeplay at Augusta, here in Blighty things are very, very different. For sheer British eccentricity there is little to beat the Sunningdale Foursomes event which is open to both amateurs and professionals and to men and women in any combination, subject of course to pretty exclusive handicap limits[5]. With the first event taking place in 1934 it was assumed that the male professionals would sweep the board. Not a bit of it. The very first winners were F Noel Layton and Diana Fishwick while Joyce Wethered and J S F Morrison triumphed in the two subsequent years.

The English Golf Union, founded in 1924 now has nearly two thousand Clubs and three quarters of a million players under its wing, simply emphasising that of all the results of the Union of the Crowns in 1603, not least was the exchange of the nations' sports. Rugby and cricket came up north and in the process passed golf on its way down – and up.

It was to be a fair exchange.

---

4   He was twice Open Champion himself, winning at Prestwick in 1887 and two years later at Musselburgh.
5   Male pros play off Plus 1, lady pros off 2. Male amateurs are off Scratch, with the ladies off 4.

THE COURT OF EQUITY

The Supreme Court of golf is constituted by R&A Rules Limited and the United States Golf Association. They jointly oversee, promulgate and every four years agree any necessary amendments to the Rules of Golf under which we all play the game. It is into their court that intractable and hitherto insoluble disputes are dragged from all over the planet and placed in the dock to receive judgement. However, where an issue does not fall within the scope of the Rules, yet directly affects the game, what then? In such a circumstance the governing bodies have, quite rightly, ordained as follows:

Rule 1 – 4 : Points Not Covered by Rules: *If any point in dispute is not covered by the Rules, the decision should be made in accordance with equity.*

So there we have it. Equity is the last stop on the road; the final swish of the curtain. However, exactly what constitutes 'equity' has remained the subject of profound philosophical debate among golfers. Deriving from the Latin *naturalis aequitas*, or natural equality or fairness, it is helpfully defined by the *OED* as 'a recourse to general principles of justice.' But what *is* justice – and *how* may I get it, is a question first asked famously by Socrates, as reported by his pupil Plato. (The answer: if you can't get a lawyer who knows the law, be sure to get one who knows the judge.)

Some say that equity is just common sense, which again just begs the question: what is sense? Is it that *a priori* knowledge which comes from the exercise of pure reason, or is it that empirical knowledge which can be generated *a posteriori* only by sensual and physical experience? As we all know, such debates rage daily in caddy huts, half-way stations and clubhouses. The whole thing is a minefield. In desperation the Old Testament was consulted, wherein we find the long suffering Job[1] crying: *I put upon me Righteousness, which covered me as a garment, and Equity was my crown. I was an eye unto the blind, and a foot to the lame.* At last, common sense from the Man from the land of Uz.

Inspired by Job, the British Golf Union is to be congratulated on the setting up of the Court of Equity. The court sits quarterly and in rotation around the countries of the British Isles to hear cases which the Rules Committees find to be *ultra vires*. A sample of the submissions and judgements which constitute its caseload are presented below:

---

1   Job : 24, v.14.

SUBMISSION: TO THE JUSTICES OF THE COURT OF EQUITY, SITTING AT YORK

May it please your Honours;

Following a major prostate operation last year, I have to wear a surgical appliance, namely an *Alert*™ incontinence pad which incorporates a loud warning buzzer. Should the pad become wet, the buzzer goes off for 60 seconds and can only be silenced by pulling out the pad and squeezing it. I have finally trained my caddy to squeeze it into silence *in situ*, but this does involve a bit of a struggle with attendant grunting and commotion.

Now, during a matchplay tie with Mr F G Hargreaves at Bagshot GC in Surrey, my nervous tension triggered a repeated loss of continence. As a result the buzzer sounded on four separate occasions, each time when Hargreaves was right at the top of his backswing. This caused increasing irritation and when the thing buzzed again on the 18th green as he was addressing a 5-footer to win, I'm afraid he exploded. He accused me of *tactical* buzzing i.e. cheating, and claimed the hole and the match.

He refused to be reasonable afterwards in the clubhouse, even pretending to be shocked when I approached him in Founder's Room with an incontinence pad and demonstrated, using a noggin of Kummel, how the buzzing was triggered.

The issue is: can a surgical appliance such as mine be deemed to be an Outside Agency or is it an Unlawful Appurtenance. The R&A say they cannot rule (surprising, given the level of incontinence at St Andrews) and have referred the case to your Court for settlement.

I am, with high consideration,

Your Honours' obliged & humble servant

R.A. Kingsbury

JUDGEMENT

We find no reference to noise-emitting incontinence pads in the published *Decisions of the Rules of Golf Committees* of the R&A and USGA. We are thus competent to adjudicate in equity and rule as follows:

Your matchplay tie with Mr F.G. Hargreaves shall be replayed. In order to restore equity between both parties, F G Hargreaves will *also* wear an *Alert*™ incontinence pad which he will be permitted to trigger, without warning, an equal number of times to yourself. This will be achieved using a concealed water bottle affixed to the inside of his trousers. In addition the party with the higher handicap will be permitted extra buzzes equal to ¾ of the difference.

In future, we recommend that you change from the *Alert*™ to the *Larkrise*™ pad which does not buzz, but emits a musical twittering identical to the song of the skylarks, such a joy on the links in summer. This is a sound at which no opponent could take offence, although by coming up from below rather than down from above, it may initially be regarded as somewhat singular.

SUBMISSION: TO THE JUSTICES OF THE COURT OF EQUITY SITTING AT PENARTH

May it please your Honours;

As you will be aware, the PGA has sanctioned the use of powerful laser rangefinders in the professional tournaments they control. These devices are apparently based on the Maser, now used by the military to fry enemy installations at great distances. At Whinfields GC we are currently having a trial of army surplus Masers during three monthly medals. The results have been unexpected. Players now carry hand-held devices while our caddies wear motorcycle helmets with GPS for rangefinding and an anemometer *cum* weathervane thing on top. The visor also has Wi-Fi and broadband so that the FTSE prices and the SPs from Kempton Park can roll continuously across the head-up display. Can this be legal?

However, and more seriously, an unknown member used his Maser to set fire to the backside of another member's plus-fours last week and is being wittily accused of arson fire, while yet another scared the Captain witless by igniting his cigar from half a mile away. This cannot go on; and there is nothing whatsoever about Masers in the Rules.

I am etc,
G E Evereard

JUDGEMENT

A Maser is of course a device for Microwave Amplification by Stimulated Emission of Radiation. A Laser by contrast is a Maser that works with higher frequency photons in the ultraviolet or visible light spectrum while the Maser operates at the longer wavelength or red-end of the electromagnetic spectrum where the frequency is lower, given the constancy of the speed of light at 300,000 Km/sec. We would have thought that this would have been clear to the modern golfer.

We find no fault with the caddy helmet described, in terms of the FTSE index and the SPs, since any advice based thereon is likely to be useless. However, we are most surprised at the use of hand-held Masers on a golf course since they produce, as your Captain discovered, not visible light waves but *microwaves* which do precisely what they do domestically in the kitchen, i.e. they fry things.

It is clearly not equitable, indeed it is quite disgraceful for a member to set fire to another player's trousers during a Medal round without due warning. Indeed, the removal by any means of a fellow competitor's plus-fours, whether by physical debagging or by the remote application of Maser radiation, is all the more reprehensible given the cost of replacement. Equally, the deliberate igniting, at very long range, of a player's cigar, cheroot, cigarette, with or without his knowledge and consent is unwarrantable since players should not smoke on the course. We find that the Maser be doused.

THE CADDY

Is there a comparable sporting phenomenon to the relationship of the golfer and his caddy?[1] Absolutely not. Well, is there *any* other comparable pairing? Possibly. There is the surgeon and his assistant, but their relationship is that of teacher and pupil, whereas with golfer and caddy it's usually the reverse. Perhaps the truest analogy is with the mediaeval knight and his armour-bearer or squire who was also a carrier of weapons. Historians report that even their battlefield dialogue was similar. The mediaeval instruction:

'The mace, methinks, Williams.' Had by the eighteenth century evolved to:

'The mashie, I think, Williams.' However the response had not changed.

'Rubbish. Ye'll be short, again. Here, tak' this long iron.'

Sadly, the old traditional pure-bred caddy is slowly passing out of existence on the linksland of Scotland, from which caddies were once exported in large numbers to the Empire. As social and indeed genetic engineering produce new strains of caddy and bag carrier, the time might be opportune to pause for reflection, as the final sunset glows behind that unique and famous outline. Come to think of it, advances in genetic science now hold out the enticing prospect of actually *cloning* a traditional specimen, thus preserving the famous characteristics of the breed. These would have to include: the flat cap or bunnet, so firmly attached to the head that its removal requires a surgical procedure; the face whose contours evoke the west coast of Ireland and whose complexion would hold three days of rain; the ancient raincoat, sometimes with pockets of the deepest suspicion; the shambling gait with its ten-degree list to port or starboard to counterbalance the clubs; the commercial morals of a Port Said secondhand rug dealer and an early morning breath which could fire a gorse bush.

The caddy's attitude towards you begins on the first tee and may be immovably fixed for the round before a drive is struck. Tommy Young, formerly my father's caddy, could take one look at me on the 1st tee and compute precisely where I had been the night before, and until when. I remember a match at Prestwick against the Trinity College men from Dublin. My foursomes partner and I had been reeled in like a pair of trout, from three up going into the famous Loop at the 14th, to all square going down the last. I then found myself lining up a nervy five-footer to halve the game. Thank God, down it went. So it was caps off, shake hands, caps on, and back across the green to face Tommy, and the music. Predictably, the roof fell in.

1 From Fr. *Cadet*: A carrier. One who ran errands in mediaeval Edinburgh.

'Well done. *Well* done. All bloody *square* when ye should've had them two an' one, if no' three an' two, and why? Ah'll tell ye why! 'It's cause ye'll no *listen*, that's why. Oh no, *you* know best. Ah've been tellin' ye and *tellin'* ye that yer grip's too strong, an' ye're still *amazed* that it's goin' left. Ye're *supposed* tae be a professor[2], but ye cannae remember a simple instruction frae one hole tae the next! An' furthermair…'

At this point he shoved the clubs at me and stalked away. I then saw him slowly come to a halt – and turn – and come back. And I thought to myself: aha, the apology. Wrong. It was the *coup de grace.*

'An' yer faither was *the same*!'

Caddies are, together with the Suggestion Book lying in that dusty corner of the Members Lounge, the most productive source of golfing stories on earth. I think it was Henry Longhurst, that great golfing journalist, who once opined that there were but four basic caddy stories, three of which had already been told. The fourth had been lost in deep rough to the right of the 16th at Birkdale in 1928 and hadn't been heard of since. They vary greatly in length and content, but caddy omniscience, waggery, roguery and above all acerbic commentary are the staple ingredients.

An English peer drove into a high gorse bank at Carnoustie and had the following immortal, scandalous exchange with his caddy who had been sent in after it.

His Lordship: 'That's *ten* minutes up, caddy. Got it?'
Caddy (*faintly*): 'Aye.'
His Lordship: 'But, is it *playable*?'
Caddy (*fainter*): 'No yet…'

They're even entertaining when absent. Once at St Andrews I was told of the R&A member who, after an Excellent Lunch[3], drove long off the first tee on The Old Course and marched down towards the Swilcan Burn. Arriving at the ball and staring forwards at the green, he said, 'Well, I reckon it's a full 9 or an easy 8. I'll take the 9.' He extended a hand for the implement. It failed to arrive.

'The 9, caddy!' he repeated sharply, hand still extended. Again no response. In great irritation he spun round but as he did so, he remembered. He had totally omitted to engage a caddy that day. It was a long, long walk back to the tee.

Now that first tee was the very one from which in 1922, HRH the Prince of Wales, who was no great golfer, drove himself in as Captain of the R&A. At each new captain's Driving In, the St Andrews caddies rush to field the ball, he who retrieves it being rewarded with a gold sovereign. When HRH came to drive in on that September day the caddies, well aware of his prowess, positioned themselves accordingly. A London newspaper reported delightedly that: 'certain of the caddies had positioned themselves disrespectfully, indeed disgracefully close to, and in one case treasonably *on* the tee.'

2   *Supposed*; A famous West of Scotland insult, implying fraud. The implication was that my entire academic c.v. was bogus and my research publications riddled with methodological inconsistencies.

3   The Excellent Lunch is one expanded in length and depth by the accompaniment of Chablis, Claret and Kummel; having a liquidity of which the Bank of England would be envious.

It was also HRH who, at Gleneagles, was the recipient of perhaps the most devastating shaft of caddy wit ever. Playing the King's Course, he was trapped in the great bunker set into the base of the hill upon which towers the first green. Pausing for breath after several (to be frank, many) increasingly desperate attempts to escape, the Prince leaned on his niblick[4] and looked up wearily to the bunker's high rim. There, glaring down, was his caddy, an old doctrinaire Marxist-Leninist republican with a predictable attitude to the House of Windsor. Said the future King to his prickly subject: 'Frightfully sorry, caddy. Seem to be a bit off form today, what?' And the old rogue, with an air of feigned total surprise, said to the still trapped heir apparent,

'Oh, so ye've played *before*, Sir?'

Of course the action can go the other way. That great American club chucker Tommy Bolt, he of the nuclear temperament, once blasted a drive away round a dangerous dogleg. The ball, as it disappeared, was last seen to be edging ever closer to the dreaded white posts. The Thunderbolt whirled round to his long-suffering caddy and snapped, 'Is that sonofabitch outta bounds?'

'I dunno, Tommy' said the caddy, wearily pulling an iron from the bag. 'You'd best throw a provisional...'

The relationship between player and caddy when both are veterans of each other, is wondrous to behold. It is not master and man, it is indeed soldier and armourer. The latter knows his man, every blade in his bag and every blade on the links. The player extends a hand. Wordlessly, the correct weapon is inserted into it. The shot departs. The blade is cleaned and replaced. The westering sun dips behind the Arran hills and the fairway hollows fill with shadow. The lights of the nearing clubhouse brighten. On the 18th green, among all the handshakes there is none warmer than between the two old comrades in arms. The armourer has been truly worthy of his hire.

Payment is made – and that, is that.

4   A lofted iron. The sand wedge had still to form in the fertile mind of Gene Sarazen.

THE GOLF WIDOW

The most famous golfing widow was of course the first one. Mary Queen of Scots, whom we met earlier, had been a widow for all of several days when the lure of the links, or of James Hepburn, Earl of Bothwell, saw her teeing it up (or teeing *him* up) at Seton Sands nearly half a millennium ago. She was not the last. Many a wife has echoed the mock Old Testament view of the game:

Behold the Golfer. He riseth with the Dawn
– and mighty are his Preparations.
He departeth in the early Hour – and is gone
an exceeding Time. But behold! He returneth
with the Dusk, smelling of excisable and
dutiable Beverages,
– and the Truth is not in him...

It is indeed a remarkable thing, and indeed a male Law of Golf that it is easier to get up at 5.30a.m. on a Saturday morning and drive 50 miles to a famous links for a 7o'clock tee-time with your mates, than to get up at 9.30 to water the cat, feed the roses or zig-zag out with the wheelie bin.[1]

Indeed the siren call of the links can induce a compliance which in some cases amounts to psychological and even physical addiction. The latter is defined by psychiatrists as an addiction so potent that failure to get a 'fix' leads to physical withdrawal symptoms and bodily disturbances. These can only be softened by re-introduction of the addicted activity or substance, and can only be cured by a programme of phased withdrawal leading to total abstinence. It has often been speculated by widows that golf itself is a true addiction and that special rehab centres should be available when the condition becomes marriage-threatening. Such a notion has hitherto been treated as a joke, but such a centre does exist. It is attached to Parkfield Golf Club an ultra-private club on the south coast of England whose address may not be revealed here. Its procedures are presently being monitored by the Department of Health prior to a decision on whether similar facilities might be sanctioned by the National Health Service.

---

1   A British device for transferring back problems from dustmen to householders.
    The only inanimate object, apart from airport trolleys and powered caddies, to have a mind of its own.

A principal concern of golf widows is usually just to establish where her husband actually *is*. Modern technology has made great strides here, as detailed in the following letter kindly made available by Maj. Warren-Dawlish, Secretary of the celebrated Royal St Luke's Club in Suffolk.

The Old Rectory
160, Racecourse Rd.
Newmarket CB8 4YF

Dear Mr. Secretary,

Do forgive me for bothering you, but have you any idea where my husband Prof. Reginald Fitzmaurice the philosopher, might be? He left for the Spring Meeting at Royal St Luke's a week ago and has not returned. I have enquired of Sgt. Maj. Watkins, your Starter, if he competed in the Meeting but was bluntly told that such information could on no account be divulged.

I understand that it was on your authority that he was recently fitted at St Luke's with an electronic tagging device which is linked to a Global Positioning System. I wonder if by this means you might be able to get a "fix" on his present whereabouts.

Incidentally, I should also like to know why he was fitted with this device in the first place. It periodically emits a loud whistling noise and its scandalously suggestive vibration is most disruptive both of our domestic and our marital relations. One would have thought that such tagging was more the province of the Probation Service than of a golf club.

Reginald is due to give a lecture at Trinity College, Oxford, next Friday on the metaphysics of Aristotle and I fear that his mind as well as his body may have wandered. I know that he was planning to discuss the text of his lecture with his empiricist caddy, Evans, who is such a help in preparing his speeches.

It may be that, lost in their discussions, they simply kept going when they reached the southerly limit of the course and hence may now be travelling south through Essex. You will recall that last year, he disappeared from your so-called Founder's Foursomes and was eventually discovered in a haystack near Farnham. Should he telephone or otherwise make contact with you, tell him that I have closed up the house and am going to my mother's – but am prepared to negotiate.

Yours sincerely,
Rosalind Fitzmaurice.

your dinner's in the dog!

ROYAL ST LUKE'S GOLF CLUB (EST. 1603)

From: *The Secretary*

Royal St Luke's Clubhouse
Carrington Magna
Suffolk SU3 1GC

Dear Mrs Fitzmaurice,

Thank you for your letter regarding your husband whose eccentricities are well known to us all here. He did play in our Spring Meeting but did not return a card and some time later we realised that he had not returned at all. A search of the course produced nothing and it was assumed that he and Evans had gone off on one of their existential walkabouts which I suspected might be continuing, as his old Bentley is still here.

You queried his being tagged. Electronic tagging was introduced in 2006 as part of our absolute determination to counter slow play. All visitors are routinely tagged, together with any member who, more than twice in one year, has been clocked at over 4 hours for a round. The tag is indeed GPS-linked, and is programmed to issue a whistled warning if more than 10 minutes elapse between shots. If the player does not speed up, a powerful vibration is generated and an automatic email is dispatched to his home, copy to me, instructing him to report to this office. The member's caddy is also tagged, but with a device which delivers a short but powerful electric shock if tardy play is detected. The big board in our Situation Room here can display the location of the player/caddy unit anywhere on the course, or indeed countrywide to within five yards.

In response to your specific question as to Prof. Fitzmaurice's whereabouts, we have just triangulated the signal from his Tag and I have to tell you that he and his caddy would appear to be in the Alamo Lounge of the Seaview Hotel in Hastings. What they are doing there, and with whom, must remain a matter of speculation since one suspects that Aristotelian metaphysics is not a regular part of the Seaview's entertainment. Good luck.

I am, Dear Madam,

Yours sincerely,
RJM Warren-Dawlish MC (Secretary)

OPEN SEASON

Another Summer, another Open. Of all the dates impressed in the golfer's mind along with birthday, current wedding anniversary, Christmas etc., few can be anticipated with more quiet satisfaction than the looming of that Thursday in July. We may change anything from our minds to our Government, we may lament the transient glance of Dame Fortune, but we know and with a powerful certainty that, come the following Sunday, we will be able to watch a man kiss a jug.

It will be a great party, as it was in the beginning. Then the aftermath of a great club's Autumn Meeting, the Open now is the Summer Meeting for old friends and foes from across the continents. There is an inescapable aura of occasion. The press arrive and hold their great annual dinner in the R&A marquee on the Tuesday. Some nervous soul, myself at Muirfield, Montgomerie at Troon in recent years, rises to propose a toast to the Association of Golf Writers; they being the most demanding, seen-it heard-it done-it bunch of journalists on the planet.

Practice resumes the next morning. Someone says something silly about someone else and is heard. There is a nascent explosion, instantly muted, for this is golf and the Open. The world recedes. The two, or one, Major winners from the US are interviewed and modestly say that this is the Biggy. And it is. The Masters is fine, the US Open divine, but the Open's the jewel for which they all pine. The Americans, well rehearsed now, don't call it the British Open in front of UK audiences, as they rightly do at home. And indeed it is The Open. From the day, a century and a half ago, when Maj. James O. Fairlie announced that the competition would be 'Open, to all the world' it has been just that. Winners have come from Africa and Australia, from America and Europa, and will come from Asia.

It will be close, as it was in the beginning. It was two strokes the first time and it could go to a playoff this year or any year – four holes comprising the greatest mental endurance test in the game. And it will have the delight of the unexpected. To take just one example from the early days: Tom Morris did not, as many believe, win the very first Open, but did win the first truly *open* Open the following year; just over a century later; Tony Lema, with time for only a single practice round, found Anderson, caddy of the absent Palmer, who simply asked the question: was he, or was he not, prepared to do *exac'ly* as he was tellt, *every* shot for *fower* roonds? He was. He did – and they won the Open.

However, it will not be as in the beginning, in the Autumn. For decades now the Open has been the highlight of high Summer with the remarkable changes in colour which prolonged sunshine brings not only to the locals but also to the links. The fairways, recently so green with the Spring growth may have turned to full brown, generating serious alarm among observers, even journalists, unused to the chameleon behaviour of British grasses. There is actually a belief in some quarters that brown grass is dead grass and that at all costs the fairways must be kept green.

This is the ultimate irony, for brown grass is live grass and asks only to be left alone for full viability and colour recovery. It is perfectly possible to play golf to the highest level on a brown Open links, such as Royal Troon in the great summer of '89 when Calcavecchia won. That week, the run on the ball was awesome. In the playoff on the final day of superb golf and the highest drama, Greg Norman saw his drive at the 18th bound on and on and finally – and fatally – into a bunker which he must have reckoned to be unreachable. That simply illustrated how course management of the golf ball on a hard brown links calls for the ultimate in skill when, as at other recent Opens at St Andrews and at Hoylake, the fairways may actually become faster than the greens. This is golf in the raw, the summer 'long game' of our ancestors brought to the peak of its uncertainty by the elements that are its soul.

And as in the beginning, there will come galleries of the watchful. Some book into hotels, some into private houses, boarding houses, B&Bs, some even prefer tents or travel on spec., but still they come. Some are in cars, some in caravans, mobile shops or on ancient motorbikes with goggled wives in sidecars. While the locals walk up, some glide down in private aeroplanes while some arrive prosperously by sea aboard the cruise liner parked off the beach by our current Walker Cup Captain. In they pour from the entire compass rose.

The tented village, now only slightly smaller than Denmark, sprawls across acres of linksland; feeding, watering, selling, abluting and generally servicing the congregation of the faith. And across that white town blows the onshore wind with its hint of sea wrack and salt spray and poetry; for amid the din below the mellifluous voice of John Betjeman may be faintly heard again, extolling the linksland with its lark song – and its splendour, splendour everywhere.

For indeed it will be at the seaside, as it was in the beginning. From that first holding at Prestwick in 1860 the Open has never gone inland. No heathland or parkland has seen the Jug. The linksland is where the game came from and it is upon the linksland that each 'Champion Golfer of the Year' shall be anointed. It will also be strokeplay as it has been from the beginning. The Amateur Championship may be strokeplay followed by matchplay, and rightly so, but the Open remains pristine. It is man against the course, the wind and the rain, and above all himself, represented by the demons in his own mind.

He and every other competitor is, save for his caddy, on his own. For unlike the other great field games: soccer, rugby, cricket, the ball is in his own court *all* the time. No competitor may touch it. Only he and his caddy can decide what to do with it. The nearest opposition may be in the same pairing but may exert influence only with their own ball. The leaderboard silently, reports the evolving fortunes of the field. The player has the option of reading it or passing with averted eyes. The rounds pass. The early unknown leader vanishes into the pack. Someone has an extraordinary score and then declines. The Bookies' favourites, refuse to shine. The eventual contenders move into position on the new leader's shoulder, just as the milers on the track close up, knowing that they have to run a great final bend, or die.

The leader comes to the last, and by this time he knows. If his caddy didn't tell him, if the leaderboard were blank, if he were so self-possessed as not to be aware, he still knows. He knows because we, who are the galleries, silently tell him. The thousands heave and swell before him. He watches from his solitude and then like a thunderbolt comes that final drive. The heads swing, a murmur grows as the fall of shot is tracked. Four to cry, five to tie and, heaven forefend, six to die.

It is, as it has been almost from the beginning, the greatest individual competition in the greatest game. It is sport as theatre and theatre as sport. And it is almost invariably good theatre. It is still open to all in the world who are good enough to qualify. Somewhere in the world this year a child will one day pick up a club – just as, one day, he will lift and kiss the jug.

ENVOI

A n *envoi* may be defined as a farewell. Traditionally it was the final stanza of a poem or a manuscript which contained a closing address to the reader for whom it was intended. This then is our farewell to you who have favoured us with a perusal of our work. It is not an adieu as we trust that we may meet again, in person next time, on some far-flung links or blasted heath. If you have enjoyed this book you are likely to be not just a golfer but, like Rafael Sabatini and hopefully ourselves, someone with the gift of laughter and a sense that the world is mad.

That world today is one increasingly enmeshed in legislation, regulation and control and overseen by bodies piously obsessed with our health & safety. Some regulation is undoubtedly necessary, such as that expressed in the celebrated, and battered, Notice in Hyde Park, shown overleaf.

Equally, regulation is required on the golf course. The R&A, combining the functions of the game's legislature, executive and judiciary, tirelessly seeks to clarify the Rules and to cope with the extraordinary situations in which we golfers find ourselves. One cannot suppress a smile at the thought of the Rules Committee opening the morning deluge of mail at St Andrews, to be confronted by demands for the position when an airshot has been delivered – to the Wrong Ball, or when a tornado removes a partner to a neighbouring county *after* commencing a stroke.

Our point is that in golf we are most fortunate in that the Rules are basically commonsensical, the etiquette conforms to plain good manners and the game itself is far more than an activity, pastime or recreation. It is a code which teaches our children perhaps the most important rule for life beyond the family; that self-mastery is the key to success and golf the key to it.

γνῶθι σαυτόν advises the lintel above the doorway to Apollo's shrine and oracle at Delphi, 'Know Thyself' and the links is the place to learn. It is surprising, indeed remarkable that the ancient Greeks did not play a game ancestral to golf. After all they invented pretty well everything else from philosophy to gardening. Perhaps on reflection it was just as well, since they'd have spent ages standing around debating the deeper meaning of it all and the pace of play would have been glacial. They did, however, give us the four cardinal virtues: courage, justice, patience and wisdom, the central qualities which the game demands.

1   Job : 24, v.14.

The book began with the evolution of Man and his greatest game. We now know that it was *ca.* 100,000 years ago that the ancestors of the European peoples left the homeland of Africa, travelled north through he Middle East and fanned out worldwide. A certain game then came to birth. Whether it came to Scotland from elsewhere is uncertain and need not detain us further. What is certain is that it later left Scotland *for* elsewhere and has taken glorious root in every continent save Antarctica – and that's just a matter of time if polar warming proceeds at the present pace.

Wherever Man has had his hands free and time on those hands he has picked up a length of wood and struck out with it. Golf thus has many parents, from China to Italy to Holland, but the lack of documentary evidence means that the precise sequence of its evolution will never be known. This is because acquired characteristics, as opposed to inherited ones, are sadly not encoded in the precise sequence of our DNA, that remarkable 3.2 billion line barcode which is the recipe for us – and you.

That has not, you may have noticed, stopped us from speculating on the game's roots. As we said in the introduction and repeat now, every statement in this book should be treated with the gravest suspicion. There are facts here of course, many of them, but there is also some of the fantasy without which we all would be sadder and greyer. So follow the advice of David Hume who was described by Bertrand Russell as the greatest philosopher ever to write in the English language. 'The just man,' said Hume 'apportions belief to the evidence.'

But what a cast of characters we have as our forbears in the game! What other sport could produce, what Monty Python sketch could describe, marching across the fairways, a parade of eccentrics such as: Colonel Bogey, Admiral Zheng, Mr Mulligan and Dr Stableford, to say nothing of: King Jamie, his royal Mum, Gen. G. Julius Agricola, C.B MacDonald and 'Titanic' Thompson. All these and countless others have swept in and then out again, leaving a trail of anecdote and story as a priceless legacy to us all.

And then there are the moderns: Bob Hope, who hit it behind a tree when playing with Eisenhower, only to find the tree trunk had two eyeholes and scuttled away at his approach; the famous pathologist who had four airshots on the lst tee at Blackwaterfoot on the island of Arran before finally losing it, literally, on his last airshot when the driver flew up from his hands to land on the clubhouse roof; the attorney at St Andrews, whose opponent's drive had felled a player on the opposite fairway, warning him (the opponent) that the way he had rolled his wrists on the backswing could be construed in Court as negligent...; and appropriately as a *finale*, the unknown Englishman who was seen marching down an Algarve beach, obviously having finally had it with golf. Bag of clubs on shoulder, he strode purposefully and silently through the surf until the Atlantic was up to his chest and then, with the tremendous bulldog determination of his race, proceeded to slowly draw each club from the bag and then hurl it powerfully in the direction of Boston – the last one being followed by the bag.

It may be thought the book has something of a Scottish lean and bias. That is not intentional, though the authors are resident in Caledonia: HD being English-educated and DWP being actually one-quarter English *via* a grandmother – and hence supporting England for the first 20 minutes of the Calcutta Cup.

Golf, unlike cricket knows no boundaries. The unified code we follow, the Rules of Golf, makes cousins of us all; just as our unwinding of the genetic code has shown that there are in fact no races, but only one, the human race in which we are all, literally, first cousins. And it is in that spirit that we should prosecute the game.

And so, dear reader, farewell. Play the course as you find it and the ball as it lies. Strike far & sure, and when in doubt about the club, take one more…

GLOSSARY: THE ABC OF GOLF

This Glossary is, regrettably, restricted by its title to A,B & C. In future editions of this work, further letters will appear as triplets as the alphabet is progressively worked through. For example, the next Edition will feature D, E & F – the Definitions of Golf – while the next will cover G, H & I – the Ghibelline (as opposed to Guelph) factions among warring mediaeval caddies. The final edition will be JKL which will explore the Jekyll & Hyde behaviours of golfers when up – and down.

A

Aim
The intended direction of a shot as indicated by a player's stance and lineup. Unrelated to the trajectory actually taken by the ball (See OB.)

Airshot
Acutely embarrassing. Caused by large galleries. The notorious Airshot Airshow on the lst tee begins with the novice golfer's very first teeshot proving to be an airshot. This is followed by another airshot 5 seconds later, then after 4, 3, and 2 seconds and so on until the club has become a blur. It ends with one last despairing airshot in whose tremendous follow-through the driver, breaking free at last, flies upwards and backwards, landing with a clatter on the clubhouse roof.

Albatross
The *second* most difficult shot in golf. A hole played in three strokes under par. Known as a *Double Eagle* in the USA, where Albatrosses are now extinct after two centuries of being mistaken for ducks by armed citizens.

N.B. The *most* difficult shot in Golf is the extremely rare 4-under par *Pterodactyl* requiring a hole-in-one at a par 5. This requires tremendous strength, a tight dogleg, frosty weather – and an old friend on the green.

Artisan
A type of restricted membership for working-class men at a great golf club. In return for hard labour and greenkeeping duties, the club indulges its artisans with a hut and several full rounds per year at any time after dark. In the days when the Lower Orders knew their place, most Royal Clubs in England had small Artisan sections. Around London during the *Luftwaffe* Blitz of 1940-1, artisans worked intensively on unexploded bomb disposal so that members might begin play by 9 a.m. Several deep bunkers at Sunningdale testify to the dangers of this work. Artisans had to obtain the club's permission to marry, but rumours that the Captain exercised *droit de seigneur* at Royal Wimblebush are a myth.

B

Backswing

That part of the golf swing where it all starts to go wrong. Studies using FMRI (Functional Magnetic Resonance Imaging) have revealed that, during the golf backswing, all the higher centres of the brain shut down. This includes both the long and short-term memory Centres, now incapable of reminding the player of every instruction received. The backswing terminates at a nebulous position known as 'the top', a position invisible to the player and, like Easter, a moveable feast. At this point there is meant to occur the mental pause advocated by professionals unaware that the memory centre is, temporarily, just a memory.

Ball

A disobedient and deviant spheroid of dimpled allure, uniform diameter and considerable expense. The only inanimate object (except the airport trolley) known to have a mind of its own. Even when struck expertly, a ball may elect to conceal itself by entering rough terrain, deep water, or an adjoining property. Actively attracted by hazards and repelled by fairways, balls are only unresponsive when pursued by desperate cries of *Fore!*

Ball-washer

(i)   A person known in upscale clubs as a caddy.

(ii) A device lurking on many tees for scouring and laundering golf balls and from which hangs a foul cloth or sullied rag. A dirty ball is inserted into the device; the plunger is plunged – or the handle rotated – a dozen times, whereupon an equally dirty and now wet object is ejected. Any lost soiling of the ball may be immediately restored by application of the rag.

Ball-marker

An intimidatory object deployed primarily to upstage opponents and, secondarily, to spot or mark a ball's position on the green prior to its being lifted for cleansing. Often a token, small denomination coin or similar object. Strategies to upstage opponents socially include having the token carry the player's family coat of arms or other heraldic device. Alternatively, the name or crest of an Open Championship links may suggestively appear. Occasionally the token will bear a tiny message such as 'smoothly, now' or 'never up – never in' in contravention of Rule 8, players being disbarred from receiving tactical advice from equipment.

Banana-ball

An extreme form of the slice. The ball starts left, then curves back before proceeding hard right into the nearest wood, watercourse or house via a closed window. The Banana Slice, formerly very severe, was greatly reduced by the celebrated European Commission Regulation (EC) No. 2257/94 of 16 September 1994 (as amended) laying down quality standards for bananas, including a restriction on curvature to 120 degrees.

In contrast, Regulation (EC) No. 1677/88 states that Class I cucumbers are allowed a bend of 10 degrees per 4 inches of length. Class II cucumbers can bend twice as much. It is anticipated that due to its greater precision, the sliced cucumber will gradually become golf's preferred descriptive vegetable.

Boomerang Hook

An extreme form of the hook. The ball starts right then curves back before proceeding hard left into an even deeper wood, watercourse or more expensive property. The Boomerang Hook, formerly very severe, was greatly reduced by a remonstrance from an Aboriginal Council in Queensland requesting that the term be restricted to a hook so severe that, like the boomerang, it actually *returned,* scattering the players on the tee. This is thankfully quite rare. It has been suggested to the R&A that the versatile cucumber (*vide supra*) Classes I & II may be brought in to serve as the universal plant descriptor for shots curving out of the park.

Bisque

A handicap stroke taken not via Stroke Indexing, but at the discretion of the player, provided he announces his intention before either party has driven off. A form of dynamic equilibration born of desperation. A variant of the bisque, not sanctioned by the R&A, is the unannounced boo. First perpetrated on Vincent Jopp in *The Heel of Achilles,* by P G Wodehouse, the higher handicapped player is entitled to shout **BOO!** twice during the round, precisely at the commencement of his opponent's downswing. Usually only one **BOO!** – delivered at the 1st, is all that is required to equalise the parties.

Bunker

A hazard under the Rules of Golf, a bunker is a natural or artificial sand-filled crater. It lies directly between one's ball and the hole, except when one's ball is actually *in* the bunker. Known as a sand trap in the US, where its function is to punish the player by trapping, or arresting the progress of his ball. American bunkers are shallow and may permit escape by the any club up to a 3-wood.

In Scotland, by contrast, bunkers are deep pits of despair. Some, known as 'pot-bunkers' are, as Bernard Darwin observed in *The Times:* 'scarcely large enough to hold an angry man and his mashie.'

In true Presbyterian Calvinist tradition, one is not punished by *being* in a Scottish bunker; one is in the bunker to *be* punished.

C

Caddie

From; proto Indo-European *Cadiaye*: A person paid to carry a player's clubs, to offer advice and to tell him where to go.

Players are responsible for the actions of their caddies who are themselves irresponsible for the actions of their players. The classical caddy exhibits a facial expression of restrained disgust, the commercial morals of a Port Said secondhand rug dealer – and an inexhaustible thirst.

Advice offered by Scots caddies is concise and blisteringly accurate. Examples include;

Oh, ye've played *before*, Sir?

Sir, hae ye thoucht at all aboot *tennis*?

Ye can play away noo, Sir. They're on the green.

Cart (aka Buggy)

A four-wheeled electrical or gas-powered vehicle for transporting two-legged, gas-powered individuals from hole to hole. Clubs which require the mandatory use of buggies on concrete tracks requiring a 50 yd. walk to and from the ball (with 3 possible clubs), are not golf clubs for, as Sandy Tatum has proposed, the game being played here is not golf – it is *Cartball*.

Also, a hand-pulled or pushed cart for the transportation of the golf bag. Now available in powered versions manoeuvred manually or by remote 'control.' The latter versions, display autonomy and are liable to proceed at pace to a river bank and halt abruptly, thereby discharging clubs into the hazard.

Casual water

Any temporary standing water visible after a player has taken his stance. Snow and ice, but curiously not steam, are deemed to be casual, as is water that overflows the banks of existing water hazards. Interestingly, this means that a raging flash flood consists entirely of casual water.

The term: *Interval* or *Comfort Break* occurring on the Programme or Menu card of a golf club Dinner and intimating a midway Intermission should be replaced by: *Rule 25, 1 (b)* which is that Rule of Golf which provides for golfers requiring relief – from accumulations of casual water...

To Club

The action of club selection. One may correctly club oneself in which case the ball proceeds the correct distance, or one may:

(i)   Underclub: in this case, despite a magnificent swing and elegantly high finish, one's ball flies like a dod of mince, fails to reach the target and falls limply into a hazard, *or*

(ii)   Overclub: here, despite an equally cultivated stroke, one's ball flies over the green, over the fence and into a cultivated field.

Overclubbing produced a memorable exchange between the young Greg Norman (Australia) and a dour Scots caddy at the "Road Hole" the famous 17th at St Andrews. Having cleared everything, Norman's approach vanished over the wall in the general direction of the University.

Norman: Caddy I *told* you it was a seven-iron not a six.

Caddy: Mr Norman, a 6-iron is no *meant* tae be hit that far…

To club his player is a principal activity of a caddy, for whom early and accurate clubbing will normally ensure a handsome tip. Conversely, inaccurate clubbing is punishable by tip-withholding and, as recently as 1930 at Royal St Luke's, by caddy rapping. This penalty, whereby the caddy was rapped across the shins, was always administered using the club which had been wrongly recommended by him, thus reinforcing the learning process.

Clubhouse

Where it all begins and ends. A structure allegedly designed for the purpose of receiving, servicing, feeding, watering and generally mollycoddling the members and the guests. Usually a haven of felicity and sometimes a storehouse of mirth, the clubhouse will also be the scene of the AGM (Annual General Mayhem) especially when the Club's proposed £1.3m. clubhouse extension, with consequent subscription hike, is up for discussion. Such meetings will normally begin with a motion of No Confidence in the chair.

Also resident in the clubhouse is the Suggestion Book, that repository of wit, invention, venom and spleen where the members can be seen in all their glory as the sources of some of the finest examples of compacted insolence in the English language. e.g. *'That a Consultant Psychiatrist be engaged forthwith, to examine the Chairman of the Greens Committee'.*

The clubhouse is, finally, home to the Secretary, or the General Manager, or the Chief Exec., or whatever the club chooses to call him. What the members choose to call him may be another matter, but here he is, the Keeper of the Trays[1]. He seems never to rest from his duties; hiring and firing; dispensing order and discipline; calming the outraged; maintaining order in Council; in summary, the indispensible dispenser of balm in Gilead.

---

1   The Captain's three legendary trays for applications for membership: Probably; Possibly; and *Never!*

ACKNOWLEDGEMENTS

We gratefully acknowledge the help, advice and assistance of the following individuals and organisations:

Archie Baird; Andrew Biggart; Roddy Bloomfield; Andrew Bowyer (for inspirational bunker play); The James Braid Golfing Society; Ian Bunch, Secretary, Prestwick Golf Club; Dr Nicholas Butler; Malcolm Campbell; Steven Chu; Champ Covington; Peter Crabtree; Colin Dalgleish, Capt., GB&I Walker Cup Team; John Davie; Ian Dalziel; Sara Dodd (for cake & homilies); Ian Dunlop; Dunaverty Golf Club; Douglas and Yves Foulis; Hamish Frew, Archivist, Prestwick Golf Club; Ian Gale; Olive Geddes, National Library of Scotland; Miranda Grant; Dr David Hamilton; Eric Hatch; The Honourable Company of Edinburgh Golfers; Angela Howe, British Golf Museum; David Joy; John Kincaid; Dr David Kirkwood; Gillian Kirkwood; Philip Knowles, Archivist, Royal Burgess Golfing Society; The Leith Rules Golfing Society; Luffness New Golf Club; Dr David Malcolm; Colin McGill; Machrihanish Dunes Golf Club; Roddy Martine; Bruce Minto; John and Jan Moffatt; Colin Montgomerie, Capt., European Ryder Cup team; Alison Nicholas, Capt., European Solheim Cup team; Geert & Sara Nijs, Holland; Guy Peploe; Pine Valley Golf Club; Linton Puckett; Dr Harry Rieckelman; The Royal Burgess Golfing Society of Edinburgh; Ed Slevin; Sunningdale Golf Club; The Duke of Strathclyde; The Scottish & Queens Universities Golfing Society; Richard Simmons, Editor, Golf International; Wallasey Golf Club; Dr Tom Weingartner, University of Chicago; Zander Williamson; Sen. Gary Wodder.

And a host of long-suffering golfing companions…

We particularly wish to thank those involved with the production of the book; Charles MacLean and Alexander McCall Smith of our publishers Maclean Dubois; Neville Moir and Hugh Andrew of Birlinn; our editor Nicky Wood and our designer Emma Quinn; and last and not least, literary agent Maggie McKernan.

Hugh Dodd and David Purdie

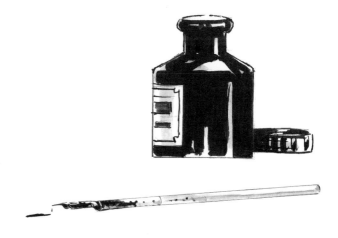

THE END